BRITAIN
POST
BREXIT

BRITAIN POST BREXIT

A PRACTICAL GUIDE TO MOVING ON

PETER McGARRICK

The History Press

Front cover image © iStockphoto/werbeantrieb

The opinions expressed in the text are those of the author alone, and do not represent the views of the publisher.

First published 2018

The History Press
The Mill, Brimscombe Port
Stroud, Gloucestershire, GL5 2QG
www.thehistorypress.co.uk

© Quicklook Books Ltd, 2018

The right of Peter McGarrick to be identified as the Author of this work has been asserted in accordance with the Copyright, Designs and Patents Act 1988.

British Library Cataloguing in Publication Data.
A catalogue record for this book is available from the British Library.

ISBN 978 0 7509 8996 1
Typesetting and origination by The History Press
Printed and bound in Great Britain by TJ International Ltd

CONTENTS

INTRODUCTION

Brexit will move Britain from the shelter of European Union (EU) membership. If the UK is to thrive, it will need to be fighting fit. Written from the standpoint of someone outside the Westminster bubble of MPs, advisers, commentators and hangers-on, this book argues that a huge number of obvious improvements can be made. A fresh look at how politics works and how problems can be tackled is badly needed.

The first part of this book is an analysis of the challenges faced in a rapidly changing world. The second part offers some suggested solutions and ways forward. In the third part we look at how these might be applied to key functions of government. Finally, the last part of the book is a vision of the UK in the years to come. Brexit will have a big impact on this; we consider how.

1

CHALLENGES

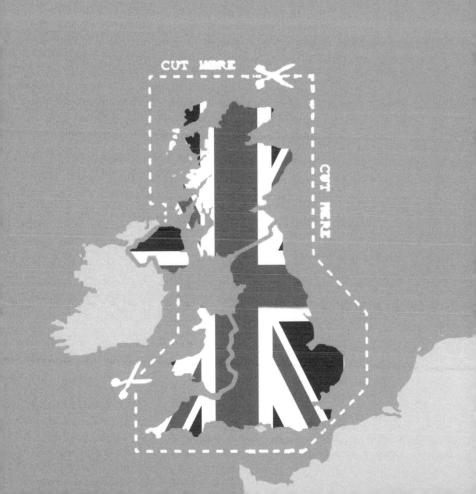

What is government for?

Someone alone on a genuinely isolated desert island would not need law at all. He would be his own government. Add just one other person and the situation is transformed. Our two people have to find ways of coexisting by developing rules of behaviour. Most of the things that we regard as crimes become possible. Matters not covered by criminal law, such as a contract or marriage, become possible. How are they to decide what rules to follow? What happens if they disagree? Or if a rule is broken?

Our islanders are now grappling with issues of law and governance. It only takes two people to generate the need for this. Consider modern society. The world has billions of people in it, with their own personalities, beliefs, hopes, fears, qualities and faults. Often, they are crowded together in quite small places. This certainly applies to the UK, and in particular England, which, if viewed as a country, is one of the most densely populated in Europe. Given the complexity of the modern world, government is not going to be easy.

Government can be viewed as a system of creating law, in order to deal with the problems facing society. Using the force of law, an administration can be effective in implementing the policies of the government. References to 'the government' often embrace the combined functions of law making and administration. In other words, the 'they' referred to when people say, 'they ought to do something about it'.

Government cannot exist in a vacuum. It needs to serve a defined group. There can be different levels of government (with subdivisions by region) but 'the government' usually refers to the one running a nation state.

Although they sometimes come and go, as a result of historical forces including conquest, subdivision and merger, nation states provide the stability required for government to work. Successful nations have characteristics that bind them together. Typically, these include some or all of established boundaries, shared culture, shared history, shared language and a general, if hard to define, sense of national belonging. Countries lacking key unifying characteristics tend to be very unstable. Law making and enforcement, and thus government and administration, become difficult.

The world as it is now

Government is about the management of people. There are plenty of them. The world population has more than doubled in the last fifty years and is predicted to grow to 9.6 billion – an increase of over a quarter – by 2050. In the UK the population has grown from 55 million in 1960 to 62 million in 2010, and is expected to be 77 million by 2050 and the largest in Western Europe.

The allocation of available resources to serve the population is a complex matter but, as we will see, one that is widely regarded as something in which governments should be actively involved. The number of people to be catered for is clearly of central importance. The relative lack of attention to this by many governments is therefore striking. Population growth and the associated pressures on resources of all kinds represent some of the world's greatest challenges.

Where efforts have been made to deal with population growth (notably in the case of China's long-standing one-child policy), the problems of sheer numbers have been supplanted by issues of demographics. China and, for other reasons, countries like Japan, have rapidly ageing populations. The relationship between the generations has the potential for tension in all societies, but especially those where the proportion of working-age individuals is low.

While population grows, in many ways the modern world continues to shrink. Distance is much less relevant than it was and almost irrelevant to the electronic communication that drives much of the modern economy. Even in relation to the transfer of goods, distance is much less significant than it was. Many high-value items (such as smartphones) are readily transportable by air. Even very bulky materials can be easily moved by sea.

Partly as a result of this effective shrinking, the tectonic plates of the world economy are shifting very rapidly. The West (which includes, rather quirkily, such countries as Japan and Australia) continues to thrive, but is being rapidly caught up by major countries, notably China, with other big ones, like India, following in its wake. Many of the developments are positive, with hundreds of millions lifted out of extreme poverty within a generation. Almost all regions of the world have shown signs of economic progress, including parts of Africa (where population growth remains a major challenge as millions of extra citizens have to be catered for each year). Someone in a hut with a smartphone and solar panel is in a very different position to someone with just a hut. The results of the change are likely to be dramatic.

It is thought that about 90 per cent of the scientists and engineers who have ever lived are alive today. One unsurprising consequence of this is ever-faster technological change.

The internet, which provides the information transfer essential to modern life, did not exist a generation or so ago. In almost every field of activity, technological advances are making transformational changes. Their impact on work patterns and people's way of life is likely to be profound.

War between nation states has not disappeared, even though formal declarations of war have become rare. Conflicts can be initiated by stealth, as happened with the incursions into Ukraine. Divided loyalties among the resident population can be used to grab territory (as happened in the Crimea and, somewhat earlier, part of Georgia). Civil wars are distressingly common and, as in the past, often vicious. Terrorism takes many forms and always seems to be with us. In recent years it has had a notably religious component.

Real pessimists can point to the possibility of world-changing natural disasters. The eruption of the Yosemite National Park in the USA is one of the favourites. An asteroid strike is another one.

And there is always the threat of disease. The Spanish Flu outbreak at the end of the First World War carried away about 100 million people. A modern plague, resistant to all treatments, would kill many more than this, in our interconnected world of routine jet travel. The associated disruption would surely lead to a very different world to today. The world may have had a narrow escape recently when the Ebola outbreak was contained with some difficulty.

There are clearly many things for a responsible government to worry about. Governments are essential. But where should they come from and how, if at all, can they be influenced or replaced?

What is legitimate government?

Government can be imposed on a population. The power of a state's internal control mechanisms can be so strong that dissent and resistance is effectively repressed, sometimes for generations. There are many past and present examples.

Strong rule from the top, passed down within families from one generation to the next, used to be the rule, not the exception. This was how monarchies operated. Some powerful old-style executive monarchies survive, notably in the Middle East, but hereditary despotism is not confined to them. North Korea takes it to the extreme, regarding its ruling family as semi-divine. Even in some theoretically democratic societies, efforts to keep the succession to power within a family can be successful.

Imposed rule is undesirable because it is dependent on repression and, as a result, is unlikely to be responsive to the needs of the people or the injection of new ideas. The benevolent dictator who uses his power to rule wisely is theoretically possible, but there are no obvious examples. Sadly, Lord Acton's comment that 'power corrupts and absolute power corrupts absolutely' is borne out by experience.

Legitimate power springs from the people. Applying this principle to create a good government is far from easy. Some selection system based on the popular will is required – in practice, this requires the use of some sort of voting system. This cannot be perfect. Winston Churchill's well-known comment, 'Democracy is the worst form of government apart from all of the others', hints at the difficulty.

There are all sorts of problems. If an effort is made to link representation to a particular area, it is extremely difficult to subdivide a country so that each vote carries the same weight. The evolution of competing parties is virtually inevitable and the support that they enjoy is likely to be uneven across a country, due to all sorts of factors that make different places different. But, if no effort is made to link elected representatives to an area, there is a strong danger of them becoming remote from those who elected them. Unsatisfactory features of the UK system illustrate how many of the problems occur in practice. We will come to these in the next section of this book.

For a democracy to work well, the voters deciding who they want to represent them need the tools to do a proper job. This requires a good flow of information and imposes a considerable obligation on the media who provide it. There are all sorts of problems here. Genuinely dispassionate coverage of political issues is very hard to find. Even organisations that try to achieve this, such as the BBC, can, consciously or otherwise, create bias via their selection of what news to cover. Many people choose to stay in their comfort zone by reading newspapers and online material that is sympathetic to the views that they already have. Tunnel vision can be the result.

The voting process itself has to be fair and trusted. Unless it is, each government is prone to being undermined by claims that it is not legitimate. Electoral fraud (e.g. 'vote early and vote often') is a concern.

Once a government is elected, what then? Is it legitimate for it to do everything that it wants? After all, the public have voted it in. Or is some measure of compromise still needed? If so, what and why? Even an elected government loses legitimacy with the passage of time. Over the years the voting population changes. Events can mean that policies become out of date.

Government is difficult. It can involve attempting to select the least bad of several unattractive alternatives. The opposition, correctly, can then point out the disadvantages of what is decided, and the popularity of the government can decline. Governments wear out, and elections need to occur often enough to refresh, but not so often that they destabilise.

Current political and economic systems

Political approaches

Persuading large numbers of people to turn out and vote for you is not easy. It is usually beyond the abilities of even the most charismatic of individuals. Very occasionally someone, with help from friends, manages to get elected. Martin Bell, the TV journalist, did this some years ago. Such people are curiosities when they get to Parliament, but they are unlikely to wield power.

The ability to form a government is dependent on being able to make laws, which is, in turn, dependent on being able to control Parliament. Under all systems, this means being able to win enough votes within the Parliament. This can only be done by co-operation, which leads to the creation of political parties.

Members of a party are unlikely to completely agree with each other about everything. If they are to work together effectively, some compromises are required. A member who feels she has to compromise too much and too often may eventually conclude that she is in the wrong party.

Parties prominent enough to have a chance of forming a government need to establish a strong public following by devising attractive policies. These can evolve. A party that has just lost an election may decide to change its tune somewhat in the hope of better success next time.

Some glue is needed to hold together a party, and this usually takes the form of some sort of political theory or philosophy. There are plenty of ideas around, so much so that they are badly served by the limited political vocabulary applied to them. This is two-dimensional in a three-dimensional world.

A key distinction (in two-dimensional speak) is between left and right. On the left, towards the extreme, it places communism. A linear progression to the right shades, by degrees, into more dilute forms of 'socialism' then to centre-left social democracy (which is more receptive to market mechanisms) until some sort of centre divide is reached. Oddly, almost no parties seem to reside in this notionally precise middle bit. Continuing rightwards, we have views increasingly placing emphasis on producing conditions suitable for wealth creation and less emphasis on welfare and state involvement.

Many commentators put fascism at the far right of the scale. This attracted much support in some countries in the twentieth century, inspired in large measure by the supposed efficiency of Mussolini's Italy in making the trains run on time. Fascism is an example of repressive government – elections stop and the secret police hunt down those who object. The state is in unchallenged control of events.

It is interesting to compare and contrast fascism with communism. Compared to fascism, theoretical communism has a much more respectable parentage. It derives inspiration from the teachings of Karl Marx in the nineteenth century. Working away in the library of the British Museum and assisted by his wealthy fox-hunting friend Friedrich Engels, Marx sought to explain the development of events, and in particular economics, with reference to mechanistic forces. In essence, there was an inevitable struggle between the bourgeoisies, who were the owners providing capital, and the proletariat (workers), who did the production. Conflict between these very distinct classes would result in the triumph of the workers over 'capitalism' (a word that Marx popularised). This would produce a society controlled by the workers, placing emphasis on the communal good, via communism.

Marx has been hugely influential, although not in the way that some of his devotees think. Before Marx the interpretation of the course of history revolved around the actions of kings and princes, generals and admirals, and their associated alliances and battles. After Marx it has become accepted that economic forces drive history. The Roman Empire (and the British, for that matter) sprang from economic power. In the case of the British Empire, this was fuelled by technological advance.

Many are attracted by the apparent purity and coherence of Marxist thought. The brief *Communist Manifesto* published by Marx and Engels in 1848 is relatively accessible, even today. More determination is required to tackle Marx's long and impenetrable *Das Kapital*, which may rank as one of the most spoken of and least read works these days. Nonetheless, notions like 'from each according to his ability, to each according to his need' have enduring force.

Particularly if explained attractively, communism/socialism has considerable intellectual, moral and emotional appeal. Its principal drawback is that it does not work.

Far more than fascism, communism/socialism was thoroughly road-tested, in different forms and in different countries, in the last century. There is not a single example of it having worked well and it has been discontinued almost everywhere. It still limps on in a few places. Much hope was invested in two of these – Cuba and Venezuela. They are disappointments. The allegation that they are corrupt, poverty-stricken dictatorships is hard to shrug off.

The failure of communism may stem from the fact that pure theory, untempered by pragmatism, does not work well in politics. Communism might work splendidly in a society of angels. It appears to have worked reasonably well in special situations, such as the early kibbutz movement in Israel, where the community involved was small and cohesive. Everywhere else, human nature seems to have polluted the implementation of the ideal.

Communist societies, such as the Soviet Union, came to have many of the features associated with fascism: repression, state control, secret police and the like. It is a matter for arid debate as to whether they were left wing – or, for that matter, whether the Nazi Party was right wing. It was, after all, the 'National Socialist' Party.

Whatever the labels, communism and fascism rank as extreme approaches that experience has shown to have produced unsatisfactory outcomes. Most political activity and attention now focuses closer to the centre ground. Clear trends have emerged here, one of which is that the range of matters that government is expected to deal with has relentlessly increased.

For much of the nineteenth century, government was reluctant to get involved with how business operated. Government paid little attention to the relationship between employers and their workers, which, as with so much else, was regarded as a matter for commercial negotiation. Society paid some attention to the poor, but this was mainly regarded as a matter for charity, not government.

This hands-off approach had extreme consequences during the nineteenth-century Irish Potato Famine. Ireland was part of the UK at the time. A million people starved. Two million more were forced to emigrate, usually to the USA, in uncomfortable conditions. Ireland remains affected by the consequences to this day. To modern eyes, the inaction of the British Government, at a time when Britain was the most powerful country on earth, is extraordinary and inexcusable. Such behaviour would now be unthinkable. But, at the time, dealing with the problem was not regarded as a function of government.

Staying, for the time being, within the restrictions of left–right terminology, it can be said that the non-intervention approach to the famine, leaving events entirely to commercial forces, was extremely right wing.

Right-wing politics aims to stimulate the growth of wealth by providing business with ideal conditions in which to thrive. To this end, there is pressure to reduce taxes and a light-touch approach to regulation of all kinds.

Moving to the left side of the spectrum, we see emphasis on intervention in the interests of the public good. We are far removed from the Potato Famine era, and government now provides support in most important areas of life, ranging from birth to death, covering health, education, welfare, transport and much else.

Modern politics, in practice, is concerned with adjusting the tensions between allowing wealth to be created while at the same time devoting resources to service the needs of the voters. Often there is far more consensus than that suggested by campaigning politicians. Changes of government often result in relatively small changes, of course.

Despite this, political debate, especially at key times such as elections, often has a childish, tribal character. Those of a different view to a party spokesperson are demonised, sometimes to the point of name calling. (In 1948, the Labour minister Aneurin Bevan described his Conservative opponents as 'lower than vermin', a mere three years after the coalition wartime government had embraced both parties.)

In the course of this unattractive process, we see the limitations of two-dimensional thinking. Antennae twitch away, sensitive to any indication of where an individual fits in the political spectrum. Once they have expressed a view on one thing (education policy, let's say), the antennae register hard left – or centre right, or whatever. This is supposed to fit individuals into the correct position on the political map. In other words, without further enquiry, assumptions can be made about their views on a range of other topics (health, foreign policy, defence …)

What nonsense this is. We are talking about ideas in a complicated world. The worth, or otherwise, of a given idea should not to be assessed via rigid left–right orientations. What matters is whether it is a good idea or not. It would be extraordinary for any individual to have nothing but bad ideas. Good ones can be found in surprising places sometimes. Their origin ought not to matter.

Economic approaches: the disruption of value

Economic activity revolves around a sense of worth, i.e. what is value? Markets, crucial to economic life, determine this. Values are changing quickly and the effect of this could be profound.

Business involves the creation or management of something of value, with a view to making money by charging the purchaser or user. The value might be in a thing, the right to buy or occupy somewhere, or a service. We are all very familiar with all sorts of examples of these. Much experience of businesses has led to a widespread, if approximate, sense of value for most of them. We know, very roughly, what we are expected to pay for a pint of milk, a filling at the dentist or a night in a hotel.

Value is important to business, but how is it assessed? Recent developments have disturbed some of the traditional sense of value. In the past, most of what people got from a business required a payment. Now, much of what people get is payment-free. This applies to a great deal of what is available online, where Wikipedia and many others provide huge amounts of information on this basis. The internet provides a lot of entertainment for 'free', or at negligible apparent cost, in the form of music, moving images, books and games.

Old economic models are breaking down. Once, a leading pop artist could expect to make large sums from the sale of records (later CDs). Some effort is still made to derive equivalent revenue in these days of online music streaming, but it is difficult. Recorded music has become very cheap, or even free. Top artists seek to make money via spectacular concerts instead, as people have to pay to get into those in the traditional way.

Has the corny old saying that 'there is no such thing as a free lunch' lost its validity? No. Google, Facebook, Twitter and other companies providing 'free' services have become huge businesses somehow. So, what is feeding them?

One obvious answer is advertising. The new platforms that they provide contain a lot of it. But there is something else, representing a new store of value. It did not exist in anything like its present form before the internet. It is called data.

Knowledge is power, and data provides a lot of knowledge. Without the public voting for it or having much of a say via other methods, in a very few years there has been an explosion in the collection and analysis of data. More and more institutions, both public and private, know more and more about us.

A modern car is likely to know where it is. This is great if you break down because help should arrive soon, but do you really want your car company to know where you drive to, all the time? Credit cards and other forms of plastic feed more information into the data system. Electronic point-of-sale technology in shops tells them what you buy. You probably file your tax returns online (more data) and your medical records are kept electronically too. CCTV, coupled with face-recognition technology, is very good at helping to catch criminals. It also, of course, captures the movements of everyone else. Modern life is virtually impossible without leaving a huge and growing electronic vapour trail behind us. You add to it with every search online, unless you are one of the savvy individuals who has a privacy setting which works properly.

The vapour trail represents a huge, and new, store of value. What you get online is not really free. You are paying for it by revealing data. This will be used for general marketing purposes ('people in Newcastle are showing an interest in black and white shirts') and sales pitches specific to you – this is why, if you do an internet search about the weather in Majorca, you soon get adverts about holidays there.

Disruption to value also takes other forms. Automated production can make goods remarkably cheap. A surprisingly large part of the cost of selling online to the consumer relates to the delivery of an item to the front door. This has to be done by a person and is therefore expensive. The relative cost of services (done by people) has increased considerably in relation to goods. Dinner for four in a restaurant can cost the same as a good TV.

However, businesses still value physical assets. If you are in the steel business, the girders in your warehouse have a value. But often this is not where the main assets of a business lie. This is not just because businesses are increasingly reluctant to tie up money in physical stock. It is because knowledge and ideas trump things, when it comes to value.

'Intellectual property' is the right to exploit know-how and things like designs and brands. Only one company can legally make Coca-Cola. Patents protect the creators of something genuinely new for long enough for them to have a realistic chance to exploit it. Patents covering certain pharmaceutical products, for example, can be of great value. This is because they create an effective monopoly (something which can be very controversial in relation to life-saving products).

The disruption of old value structures has had a major impact on how businesses, and thus economies, work. The old model involved a lot of people being employed in tasks of varying complexity, in order to make things. The end products represented a store of value for the business, which would try to make money by selling them.

A great deal of modern business looks very different. Manufacturing can require very few people. Often there is no 'manufacturing' at all. The store of value is nothing like a warehouse full of girders. It is a will-o'-the-wisp – the right to exploit intellectual property. If the 'product' is something like an app or an ebook it is, in physical terms, really thin air. Retaining and protecting value is becoming much more difficult. You can guard and protect your girders, but preventing someone from stealing your industrial design, perhaps by reverse engineering your product in somewhere like China, is much more difficult.

Unsurprisingly, employment patterns have changed. Far fewer people are engaged in physical production and much employment is now in services. But there are other changes. The crucial importance of the value of ideas, captured via intellectual property rights, puts a premium on the services of their creators. Automation and computerisation do much of the grunt work. People are still needed for certain things (such as delivery) but much of the work specific to humans is relatively mundane.

A polarisation is taking place. At the top of the pile is a small elite of creators, business managers and high-end professionals. At the bottom are the caterers, office cleaners, despatchers and the like. The need for people in the middle, in clerical and middle-management roles, is reducing.

Economic approaches: business structures and ownership

Everything has an owner. Sometimes it is the state. Businesses have owners (including, sometimes, the state). Ownership can take a number of different forms. Often the owner is an individual, whether operating as a one-person business or employing one or more others. Partnership arises when two or more people operate a business in common with a view to making a profit.

Britain, and particularly England, home of the common law, has been very influential in evolving business structures now widely adopted around the world. One of the earliest and most spectacularly successful (not to say rapacious) was the East India Company. Originally formed by royal charter, this evolved, in the course of a colourful and controversial history spanning several centuries, into a highly profitable business with shareholders, many of whom became wealthy as a result. Along the way it did much to build up British imperial power, especially in India.

The East India Company can be viewed as an early example of, and/or the forerunner to, a multinational business. Its operations were so extensive and its geographical reach so broad that it was hard for a national government, even a powerful one like Britain's, to control it.

The East India Company had a 'legal personality'. In other words, it was separate from its owners. All limited liability companies share this crucial characteristic. Large or small, they make contracts, pay their taxes and do all sorts of other things independent of their owners. This is very different from the position of sole traders and partnerships. Limited liability companies do what they say on the tin. They limit the liability of the shareholders. The company can go bust but the shareholders only suffer the fact that their shares become worthless.

The attractions of company status mean that almost every large business trades as such, together with many small ones. A huge banking and finance sector (which in itself represents a significant slice of business activity, especially in the UK) has grown up to service the requirements of companies. There is cradle-to-grave attention as serried ranks of often highly paid professionals attend to their creation, nurturing, development and, if need be, sale or termination.

Since so much economic activity is dealt with by companies it is worth looking under the bonnet to see how they work. Like any business, money is needed. This can be provided by the shareholders, who are the owners, or it can be provided by loans, usually from banks. Very often a business gets money from both of these sources.

Someone has to run a company. At least one 'director' is needed, although big companies almost always have several of these, often with specialised roles (such as finance, production or marketing). They, plus other managers who are not directors, operate as the mind of the company and control what it does – subject to one thing.

It is the shareholders who own the business and, in theory at least, have the ultimate control over it. This almost never gets them involved, in their capacity as shareholders, in any day-to-day business decisions, or even major ones ('Shall we close the factory in Huddersfield?'). Nonetheless, shareholder approval is needed for important things, such as decisions to sell the company which they own, issue more shares, and other matters relating to its structure and ownership.

We have identified two groups of people involved in the operation of a company – its owners and those who work for it. But there are others very much involved. They are the customers of the company and members of the public at large ('society', if you like). A good economic and political system will create a good relationship between these four groups – owners, workers, customers and members of society.

The present arrangements can be improved upon and we will consider how, later in this book.

State ownership of a business removes (or at least replaces) one of these elements (the private owners). We will consider if this works well and whether there are better ways of reflecting the interests of society as a 'stakeholder'.

Culture, religion, philosophy and morality

A society needs something to hold it together. Physical boundaries alone will not be enough. Without more, tensions between different groups will lead to disintegration, possibly even civil war. The relative stability of nation states allows integration of various kinds to develop. It is needed in order for people to get along well enough for a country to function. There has to be at least some togetherness.

A common language, while not essential, can be a very important connecting factor. Unless members of a society can communicate easily there are likely to be barriers between them. Shared experiences, stemming from the fact that people are living in the same place, subject to the same laws and perhaps external pressures from other countries can help. Nothing tends to unite a country quite so much as an external threat, which can be war, in an extreme case.

History, as past shared experience, can play its part. Even though few people in the UK are old enough to remember life during the Second World War, the country was shaped by the experience of it in a way that still resonates today. Britain is different from France and Germany, partly due to this.

Shared experience takes many forms, including education: 'Nothing in life shall sever the chain that is round us now', to quote the Eton boating song. There is a strong sense that the formative years of childhood shape us for the rest of our lives. Cultural inputs of all kinds, including entertainment and sport, are part of the mix.

We all need to be a bit philosophical as we stroll along the great banana skin of life, and religion and/or philosophy shape society as well. They are key to the formulation of a moral code, which in turn feeds into the creation of the laws that society needs in order to regulate itself in an orderly way.

It is neither essential nor desirable for everyone to have the same perspective on life. The consequence of that would be a drab monoculture. Societies that come close to this are intolerant of other views and thus aggressive: think North Korea or 'Islamic State'. Enough cohesion is nonetheless required to avoid troublesome disintegration, and striking the correct balance between this and repressive conformity is one of the challenges of society – and therefore government.

Lifestyle and work

Traditionally it was realistic to follow an occupation throughout a working life. Surprisingly, often this was with the same employer. The long-term nature of the relationship was often reflected in pension arrangements. People could stay in much the same job, ticking off the years, until, following a stilted leaving party and a couple of glasses of warmish white wine, they started to enjoy a company pension, paid with reference to the number of years of service and their final pay level. Public sector employees (civil servants and people in the health service are examples) still enjoy these benefits, and often many years of uninterrupted service.

Modern life has brought many benefits, but alongside them much of the old stability has been lost. Banking is an example. Branch staff in a bank used to have a steady career path with a reassuringly solid employer. Now branches are closing and staff numbers being cut as retail banking increasingly shifts online.

These changes are modest compared to other walks of life. Elsewhere, entire industries have been swept away, or dramatically shrunk, including coal mining, shipbuilding, textiles and much more of Britain's once-dominant manufacturing industry.

Life involves a great deal apart from work. We consider how it can best fit into people's lives in the next part of the book.

Business structures

We have already identified the four groups affected by the operation of a business: owners, staff, customers and wider society. Current company structures only recognise a small part of this mix. This concerns the relationship between the managers who operate as the controlling mind of the business and the shareholders who own it.

This problem is particularly acute in the case of the largest businesses (which, because of their size, are in some ways the most important). Major companies, whose shares are bought and sold on stock exchanges, very often have a large number of shareholders. To that extent they are labelled 'public companies', even though the general public have no involvement, apart from those individuals who own some shares. There are disadvantages to this. There can be a shortage, or even complete lack, of shareholders with a sufficiently large stake to have any influence over the conduct of the business. The theoretical ability of the shareholder owners to hold managers to account, via votes in company meetings, remains just that.

There is a sense of remoteness between shareholders and the management. It is compounded by the fact that shares are routinely held through a whole host of investment funds. Individuals, and their pension providers, often put their money into varied funds, rather than having too many eggs in one basket in the form of a shareholding in one business. Another reason for lack of engagement by shareholders with a company that they partly own is that shares in public companies can be bought and sold easily. Poor performance by a business results in shareholders (often fund managers) voting with their feet and selling up. It is rare for them to hang on in there and talk things through with the management with a view to sorting things out.

In a small business, a committed owner, with her money at stake, is likely to stay the course and help to improve matters. The bigger the enterprise, the less likely that is to happen, as the numerous 'owners' skulk, largely impotently, in the background.

In short, the mechanisms of control are usually not working well. Managements get on with operations more or less as they see fit, typically awarding themselves high rewards in the process (which the business has to pay for). In recent years this seems to have got out of hand. Top managers now earn rewards which represent a disproportionate multiple of the average for their company staff. Understandably, this fuels an 'us and them' resentment.

So far as the relationships that the business has with its workers, customers and society at large is concerned, company structures have almost no role. The slack has to be taken up by the general law, via extensive provisions governing employment rights, consumer protection, environmental legislation and the like.

International relations

Britain, it is often said, is an island. Its history, however, is anything but one of isolation or introspection. Few, if any, countries have the same record, going back many centuries, of pushing back boundaries, seeking new connections and stimulating trade. As a result, English is the international language of commerce, the common law is the world's most successful legal system, particularly in the world of business, and there is a residue of connections spanning the globe that is the envy of many. Until fairly recently, the UK was one of a small number of countries capable of exercising powerful military reach, if need be, far away.

For all the above reasons, the UK has long experience of being 'a player' on the world stage. It remains one of five permanent members of the Security Council of the United Nations (viewed by many as a sort of 'top table' in world affairs). It belongs to other groupings – or talking shops – such as the G7 (the countries with the biggest economies) and the often-neglected Commonwealth.

The world is changing fast. There are growth pains, tensions flowing from change, clashes of culture and good old-fashioned rivalry. Competition for resources, ranging from water to key commodities such as copper and lithium, represents part of the mix.

Different societies offer very different solutions to the challenges of government. These spring from their own history, culture and circumstances. If you are trying to run China, should you follow the Western democratic model? Those currently doing the job don't think so.

The creation of the United Nations (UN) in 1945 represented an earnest attempt to improve on the previous, largely unregulated, way of dealing between nations. Agreements between countries (treaties) can set up 'supranational' institutions and the UN is the biggest of these. Almost all countries are members and the institution is a major source of international law.

Public international law (which covers countries, not individuals) differs from other law in that it is often very difficult to enforce. A country determined to ignore the rules (as UN member North Korea regularly does) can do so for years, possibly forever. Despite this, international law, including things like Security Council resolutions targeting apparent infringements, has considerable impact. There may be lawbreakers around, but the position is still better than having no laws at all.

The concept of a supranational law-making body has developed considerably in recent years, never more so than in the case of the European Union. As we know from the Brexit vote, getting the relationship between such a supranational entity and its member states right can be a challenge. Let's add that to our list of challenges and move on to the next section of the book, which suggests some solutions.

2

SOLUTIONS

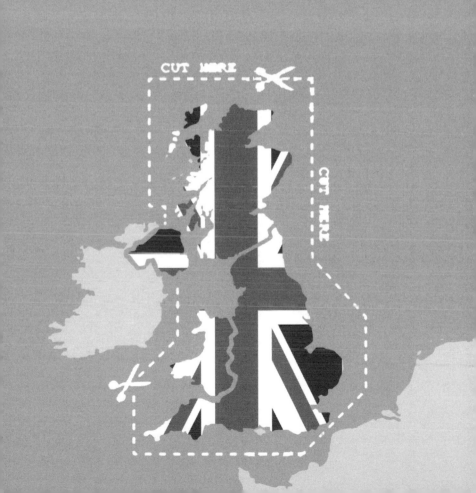

Society: some governing principles

What principles should our lawmakers follow? How much law is needed and what forms should it take? Apart from law-making processes, what else do we need to make society work properly?

Different systems of law have different starting points. In England and Wales (but not really Scotland or Northern Ireland) we have the common law. This has grown over centuries from very obscure beginnings. It is added to when Parliament passes new laws, but also via consideration of law by the courts. The common law has a practice of following precedents set by important courts. If cases are similar, then they will, due to the concept of following precedent, be decided the same way. There are gaps in the law and many grey areas. These are dealt with in court decisions. Over time, precedent-based, judge-made law has become significant. As an example, much of the law of negligence, which gives rise to the ability to make all sorts of claims, is judge-made law.

One feature of the common law is its underlying assumption that anyone is free to do whatever they want to, unless the law prevents it. This is an important philosophical approach which, due to the importance of law in underpinning society, has considerable significance.

'Civil law' countries, which include almost all EU member states but not the UK and Ireland, approach matters differently. Deriving inspiration from the Romans (who were no slouches when it came to setting up systems that lasted), they are code based. Napoleon was very taken with the idea and the resultant 'Code Napoleon' has proved very influential in more modern times. The idea is that if you want to know what the law is, you can look up the relevant bit of the code.

However, gaps in the code give rise to concern – suddenly it appears that something is lawless. There is no common-law-style acceptance of such a position to be resolved, if need be, by judge-made law in a precedent-setting case. Instead, there is a feeling that 'unregulated' is much the same as 'illegal'.

The common law approach is, surely, to be preferred. It is instinctively libertarian, not authoritarian. Building on this idea, it can be argued that something should only be made illegal when there is a strong reason for it to be so. The fact that many people dislike it (fox hunting, or nude sunbathing, perhaps) should not of itself make it illegal. The criterion ought to be the prevention of significant harm, not the prevention of causing offence, unless that is so serious that it results in significant harm. We should not live in a confining society whereby anything disliked by a sufficiently large group is banned, simply because they don't like it. That is the path of intolerance. It leads to tensions. It does not lead to a feeling of living in a 'free society'.

There is wide acceptance that things like murder and rape should be crimes. Indeed, the list of serious crimes is a long one.

Much law is 'civil', in the English sense of the term (i.e. non-criminal) and regulates interaction between individuals (and businesses). It gives rise to claims in the civil courts for all sorts of things, such as breach of contract or negligent driving. Is there scope for and a need for some third strand of law, between full-on criminal law and civil law?

A tentative go at this third strand occurred a few years ago with the development of the 'anti-social behaviour order' (ASBO). This was an attempt to deal with difficult social issues without involving the full weight of the criminal law.

The range of conduct dealt with by ASBOs was broad, including begging, vandalism, noise, joyriding and much else that a neighbourhood could do without. However, experience of ASBOs led to disappointments and the system, as originally set up, has morphed into something a bit different. The underlying causes of the behaviour being dealt with are various and difficult to deal with (mental illness, drug taking, gang culture, deprivation). It is no surprise that the attempts to set up a 'third strand' of law have had problems.

Despite the difficulties, there may well be scope for it in certain cases where the conduct involved is undesirable enough to require some official response but not enough to justify criminal sanctions. Let's keep an eye on our nude sunbathers. Can we normally leave them in peace, but step in if they are going too far, for example by using a park next to a school?

Any third way mechanisms need some form of enforcement. Community service orders and even fines might be imposed if need be, without creating the stigma of a criminal record. The law cannot and need not deal with everything. Good manners help to oil the wheels of society everywhere. Social pressures can be very effective in encouraging them. The more cohesive a society, the stronger these tend to be. Conversely, challenges arise if different groups have very different ideas as to what counts as acceptable behaviour.

Society cannot expect government and the courts to iron out every tension or problem. For it to work well there needs to be considerable tolerance of differences. Communication and mutual understanding are important here. Insofar as Britain has insular groups, especially if they are unable or reluctant to speak English, this is a recipe for problems.

Religion also has a significant part to play. All main religions offer up a rich cultural and philosophical soup. Much teaching is centuries old, having impressively stood the test of time. Many derive comfort and inspiration from the teachings on offer. But religion is divisive. The faiths differ.

Since great issues of life, creation and morality are covered, infused in many cases with a very strong sense of divine inspiration, the feelings generated can be very strong indeed. Once convinced that a particular perspective is the right one, a person can find other views to be an outrageous denial of God. It can then, for some, be a short step to express hatred of 'unbelievers' (i.e. anyone with a different perspective) in an extreme way – perhaps up to, and including, blowing them up.

We have laws against blowing people up. They have their uses and relevance, but the law alone cannot do the job required. The need for tolerance and mutual understanding applies to religions – especially now that religious-inspired murder is perceived to be on the rise. As with other areas of tension, communication is vital.

Separation militates against communication. Given the fact that childhood is the base from which we grow, it is unfortunate that separation caused by religion-based schools is tolerated. A wonderful opportunity to mix people up at a crucial stage in their lives is perhaps missed.

We have considerable experience of what can happen in the UK. Even within the same religion, the division between Catholic and Protestant schools in Northern Ireland has had long-term and serious effects on society there. It still has the obscenity of huge walls in Belfast and other places to keep 'the communities' apart. Here some progress has been made, with the creation of some 'integrated schools'. This surely shows the way forwards and has applications elsewhere.

Diversity in society is very valuable. Just as a painting benefits from the application of a varied palette, so a wide range of views and cultures helps the nation to thrive. Having absorbed people from so many different places for millennia, Britain enjoys a particularly rich mix. At the time of the 2005 London bombings, Ken Livingstone, the then mayor, was able to point out that the city was home to citizens of more than 160 countries, speaking about 200 languages.

Britain's ability to absorb new arrivals is better than many suppose, although our record is far from perfect. Success depends on tolerance, communication and adaptability. Some would claim that these are among our national strengths. Newcomers must play their part, not least by learning English and familiarising themselves with the fascinating and rather extraordinary country that they are joining.

Everyone is entitled to join in discussions about how to use the government to shape society.

Let's talk about politics differently

Is there a better way of approaching how we discuss political issues? Yes. Can we break away from the tired old structures of left and right, with the associated tendency to trap ideas in boxes only available to those regarded as believers in the relevant orthodoxy? Yes.

Labels matter, partly because they can constrict thought. They can become out of date. Consider the names of our two main political parties. Would you now pick the 'Conservative Party' as a name? I suspect not. It suggests a backwards-looking, stick-in-the-mud mindset. The 'Enterprise Party' would surely be better.

What about the 'Labour Party'? This is redolent of downtrodden workers leaving a mill in an L.S. Lowry painting. Some might regard them as promising 'class war' protagonists, but the image is one of a world that has gone and will not come back.

In his book *Chavs*, political commentator Owen Jones wrote:

> A return to class politics as it was practised and preached in, say, the 1970s would not be appropriate. After all, the working class on which it was based has changed fundamentally. The old smokestack factory skyline has gone. With it has disappeared (or is rapidly disappearing) the largely male, industrial working class ... A new movement has to speak to a more fragmented, largely non-unionised workforce.

'Enterprise' is often (and sometimes justifiably) associated with initiatives taken by individuals, who provide the spark needed to get things going and the drive to see them through to completion. The Labour Party puts emphasis on co-operation in the interests of society at large. It is a more collective mindset. Its validity is not dependent on the continuation of 'dark satanic mill' employment structures. A better modern name would be the 'Co-operation Party'.

'Enterprise' and 'co-operation' do not have to be never-the-twain-shall-meet polar opposites. On the contrary, they both have valuable features. This gives us a clue as to how to find appropriate solutions to the issues of the day. Although the two main parties have, between them, had a near monopoly of power for a century, there are other players on the political landscape.

The Liberal Democrats at least have an inoffensive, if not very informative, name. Traditionally patrolling the waters of the centre left, they face a challenge in seeking to be distinctive, and not just a somewhat more rural version of the Labour Party. Brexit presents them with an issue to seize upon. (There will be more on Brexit later in this book.)

Newer parties have names that tell you what they are about. The Green Party has sisters in many countries and, as the name implies, a strong focus on environmental matters. It is the one UK party comfortably in step with its counterparts elsewhere in the EU. The Scottish and Welsh Nationalist parties have been instrumental in securing powerful assemblies in their respective countries, reflecting concerns that the Westminster Parliament was too centralised and remote. The United Kingdom Independence Party (UKIP) operates under a name that requires little explanation. As with the nationalist parties, it is an example of a new strand of political thinking that has helped to bring about significant change – in the form of the Brexit vote, of course.

The arrival of effective, relatively new, parties has altered the political scene. It is not always sensible to casually apply the old political terms. For example, Scottish Nationalist policy has sometimes managed to outflank Labour on the 'left', but 'National Socialist' is neither a comfortable, nor appropriate, label. We need to enrich and free up our political vocabulary – and more importantly, our thinking.

Who gets what? Wealth distribution

Since most of what the government wants to achieve involves spending money, often a great deal of it, the distribution of society's material resources, and the ways in which government can influence it, are a major preoccupation. All parties have strong views.

A focus on enterprise: capitalism

Before wealth can be distributed it has to be gained. The world is not a fair place and some individuals, via inheritance, luck, endeavour or a combination of these, become rich. It is a bit flippant, but not necessarily inaccurate, to say that this reflects how the world – and nature – works. The powerful thrive and others do less well.

In an economy in which enterprise can prosper, large fortunes can be made. Attracted by this, many are incentivised to give things a go by investing and/or borrowing money, perhaps employing people, often working hard and certainly aiming for success. In the internet era, there have been spectacular examples of this, as Bill Gates (Microsoft), Steve Jobs (Apple) and Mark Zuckerberg (Facebook) built up businesses from small beginnings that have made them tens of billions of dollars. It is notable that they all did this in the USA, signalling that that country is, as it claims, a place where enterprise can thrive.

But is this a desirable state of affairs?

Not everyone thinks so. The resultant glaring inequalities are highly objectionable to many people. Rupert Murdoch, a far from popular multibillionaire, expressed the tensions as follows: imagine two poor people seeing a rich man drive past in a nice car. One might think, 'Come the revolution, mate, we'll soon have that off you'. The other might think, 'If I work hard, I might have a car like that one day'.

A focus on society: communism

What is the point of having huge wealth? However rich a person is, they can only eat so many fine meals a day, only occupy one property at a time, only drive in one car at a time, etc. Very wealthy individuals have several houses and cars – perhaps even several yachts and aircraft. This seems to be an abysmal misallocation of resources. Surely it is offensive when there are countless people in society who are very disadvantaged?

It is open to a government to step in and even things up. Wealth can be taxed, or even confiscated. The money thus gained by the state can be passed on to the needy.

This seems to be a good idea. It is not a new one. So, what happens when it is tried in practice?

There are numerous examples because that is what happened in communist societies. Consider Russia. In 1917, a communist government displaced the old aristocratic regime in what had been a hugely unequal society, with a small, very wealthy elite and a huge, very poor peasantry. Personal wealth was snuffed out easily enough. However, the conditions of the peasantry remained dire.

Russia (which morphed into the Union of Soviet Socialist Republics, or USSR) is an enormous country which, whatever political philosophy is being applied, certainly requires government. A few early efforts to manage things via an idealistic pooling of resources (including spouses, in certain cases) failed to take root. The proletariat did not suddenly convert into a wonderful agency of unselfish government. Someone had to take decisions. Members of the Communist Party did.

In the early days of the USSR there was much to do, not least fight a nasty civil war against White Russian forces trying to re-establish the old way of doing things. The Communist Party took an iron grip. Things were going to be done their way – dissent was not allowed.

Following the death of Lenin, the one-time prophet of the communist approach and the first leader of the USSR, in 1923, the enormous apparatus of government was taken over by a new man, who styled himself Joseph Stalin. Stalin's personality no doubt had much to answer for in what followed, as millions died of starvation and disappeared at the hands of the secret police and operators of *gulag* prisons, which all too often had the character of death camps.

Surely others could make a better job of realising the communist dream? After the Second World War, plenty of people tried. Communist regimes took root in all of Eastern Europe, China, Balkan states like Yugoslavia and Albania, and significant parts of the Far East. References to the Cold War relate to decades of competition between these societies and Western ones, which followed the enterprise model.

The boundaries were sharp, none more so than in Berlin. Divided at the end of the war, the city was split between its flourishing Western areas and East Berlin, which had been the Russian sector and became the capital of the communist state of East Germany.

The Germans are a productive lot and East Germany made better progress than many communist economies. Half-time in the Cold War gave a good clue as to how things were going. The contrast between thriving West Berlin and its communist counterpart was so stark that in 1961 a wall was built to keep the East Berliners in. This monument to failure was still there when I visited Berlin with my German wife in 1990. The outcome of the Cold War struggle was plain to see. The East German Government was moribund. Reunification with the West was a few months away. Thanks to courageous East German people power, the wall was already a relic. It was possible to move through it unhindered (provided you paid 15 East German marks if you were a foreigner).

Walking the streets of East Berlin that sunny Saturday was quite an experience. Forlorn little light blue Trabant cars spewed blue two-stroke emissions from their tiny exhausts. Sleek black Mercedes, crossing the border for the day, purred past them. The symbolism was obvious. It was unseasonably warm, and a beer would have been nice, but this was a communist city on a weekend – nowhere was open.

A visit to Potsdam, then part of East Germany, was like a jump into a time warp. Prosperous, by East European standards, the shops were full of stuff. The Eastern bloc goods on offer looked as if they had come from an earlier age.

There is not a single example of communism producing economic success comparable to that in established enterprise societies. Except for a handful of holdout countries like Cuba and Venezuela, it has been abandoned. Does this mean that it is hopeless for a government to try to do something about gross inequalities in society, between rich and poor? No.

Enterprise and co-operation

The obvious failures of full-on communism do not mean that there is no useful place for a co-operative – or collective – approach. It is as if attempts to apply pure communism act like the administration of a very powerful drug. An overdose can be extremely damaging.

'Social democracy' administers the drug in very much more dilute doses. Instead of appropriating all assets and then reallocating them as those in control of the state see fit, enterprise is allowed to continue in some form. However, instead of being allowed to operate entirely freely, it is constrained in various ways and *some* of the fruits of it are taken by the state.

Nearly all countries now follow this sort of model. Political activity substantially revolves around debate about fine-tuning it. The decisions taken have a major impact on people's lives and so it is important that the machinery of government which enables them to be taken works properly. How do we ensure that?

Find your demos

The UK seeks to operate as a democracy. Ancient Greece is credited with early explorations of the democratic approach and this took the form of a city-state government, where citizens were entitled to have their say in decision making. '*Demos*' can be a reference to the common people of an ancient Greek state. The word 'democracy' derives from it.

More recently, the concept of demos is used to identify the populace of a democracy as a political unit. While it may not be an easy exercise, getting the political unit right is clearly important to the proper functioning of what we are seeking to achieve – good democracy. It needs to be small enough to respond to the popular will, but large enough to be an effective government unit.

As with nation states, a minimum degree of cohesion is desirable. If those within the 'political unit' do not sufficiently share circumstances and aspirations, it is hard to see how the politics governing it will work well.

Parliament needs to be reformed

The UK is an established state and, as such, has a clearly defined demos. Political parties are well entrenched, albeit that the system is sufficiently flexible to accommodate new ideas (Scottish and Welsh nationalism, green politics, UKIP). But even if we are happy with our identification of the UK as a workable demos, does this mean that we enjoy an unimprovable democratic system? No.

The Palace of Westminster remains functional as the home of the British Parliament, but after many years of operation it is crumbling and in need of major refurbishment and change. This is an uncomfortable metaphor for the institution it houses. Major improvements are needed. As disconcertingly large sums are spent to sort out the physical fabric, the opportunity should be taken to make changes to the institution. So, what should be done?

Features of the present system include a first-past-the-post way of returning elected members to the House of Commons.

A major consequence of this, and arguably a significant benefit, is that everyone has 'their MP'. The notion that MPs are sent off by their constituents to represent them has genuine substance and there is a long and creditable record of MPs helping their constituents in all sorts of ways. Importantly, this is regardless of the voters' political views.

If something significant is likely to happen (such as the construction of a high-speed rail link) the local MP will be expected to speak up for her area. Part of the motivation, of course, is a wish to be re-elected in due course. This connectivity between the citizen and government via an MP would be lost if voters simply chose a party to vote for and then several members were returned, in accordance with party priorities, as happens with a proportional representation system (PR).

Another claimed advantage for 'first past the post' is that it squeezes out small, weak parties and leads to strong governments able to implement the policies they promised voters when they sought power. Countries which operate PR normally have coalition governments. This routinely means that the resultant policy is a compromise. That may or may not reflect the wishes of much of the voting population, but almost inevitably any coherent programme promised in a campaign never passes into law. There is also a risk that, in order to keep a coalition together, difficult issues are avoided. 'Lowest common denominator' government may not be good.

There are huge problems with our first-past-the-post system. If we accept that each vote should carry the same weight, it is hopeless. In practice, for many reasons, most seats contested at elections are safe seats. In other words, it is pretty obvious which party is going to win. That means that voters in those constituencies have virtually no influence on the outcome. Real voting power is confined to the 25 per cent or so of constituencies where the outcome is in genuine doubt.

Another problem is that the result of elections can be monstrously unfair. In 2005 and 2010 the Liberal Democrats won about 22 per cent of the vote, which translated into a mere 9 per cent or so of the seats. In 2015, UKIP, then near the height of its popularity, won an impressive 13 per cent of the votes but only one MP. These outcomes came about because support for these unfortunate parties was widespread. The position would have been very different if it had been geographically concentrated. (As for the Scottish National Party spectacularly in 2015, when it won fifty-six of fifty-nine Scottish seats in the Westminster Parliament.) Again, we see a departure from the ideal that every vote should have the same weight. If you are where your party has special strengths, your vote counts for more.

If the method of filling up the House of Commons looks unsatisfactory, it is excellent compared to the major embarrassment presented by the House of Lords. The British constitution is unwritten. Like the common law, it has developed over centuries. The House of Lords is a relic. It harks back to the time, centuries ago, when aristocrats helped to call the shots by virtue of their position in society, based on the hereditary principle.

Starting with Earl Grey's Reform Act in 1832, via extensions in 1867, 1884, 1918 (votes for some women), 1928 (women vote on the same basis as men) and 1970 (the voting age lowered from 21 to 18), elections to the House of Commons covered the British demos. The contrast with the unelected House of Lords became increasingly stark.

By stages its wings have been clipped, to the extent that it is now supposed to be solely a revising chamber. As such, it can be remarkably good, polishing rough edges from what is produced by the Commons. But clipping the wings of the Lords has not led to a satisfactory situation. The Lords can still cause a flap, not least because of a residual ability to delay the creation of new law. (This is not supposed to happen to financial measures, although what counts as such can be a bit unclear sometimes.)

There is wide agreement that reform is needed and there have been numerous proposals. They have all got stuck in the mud. A major reason is that the Commons like a weak 'upper chamber'. The moment members of the House of Lords gain legitimacy by being elected, they will acquire fresh wings and seek to take law-making flight.

Because of a system of appointment, coupled with a reluctance to retire, the Lords has an absurdly large number of members. It is one of the most bloated chambers in the world. In its favour, it must be said that one reason why the Lords continues to stagger on is the very high calibre of some of its members. Its role as a revising chamber is enhanced by the presence of highly experienced individuals, including those who used to hold high office (in the Commons) and people who are highly expert in their own field and not political at all. (The major parties vote on party lines in the Lords, but these members are independent 'cross-benchers'.) Nonetheless, all in all, the House of Lords is not fit for a country claiming to be the proud home of 'the mother of parliaments'.

Under the British constitution, no law proposed by Parliament passes into law until it has received the Royal Assent. This was last refused in 1708 by Queen Anne. A refusal nowadays would unquestionably trigger a constitutional crisis. We have the shell of the old procedure, but not the substance inside. We have a 'constitutional monarch'.

Passions run high sometimes in relation to the monarchy. A constitution starting from scratch would not select a hereditary monarchy to fulfil the role of head of state. Critics say that, in the twenty-first century, it represents an unacceptable symbol of undeserved privilege.

Not everyone agrees – including other countries where the queen remains head of state for them. Arguably, considerations of constitutional purity ought to be trumped by considerations of what works. In an age of image and branding, viewed as a brand, the British monarchy is in the top league. The queen has almost certainly met more world leaders and people of prominence than anyone else on earth. Her status as monarch is part of the reason, not just her long reign. Who wants to meet the President of Germany? Or even knows who he (or she) is?

Whether people like it or not (and many don't), a lot of stardust clings to the royal family. Replacing our world-famous and charismatic monarchy would be like abandoning the brand Rolls-Royce and replacing it with 'Snibbo'.

A new constitution

Here goes …

Change is disruptive and too much change unnecessarily so. There is no such thing as a perfect system. What follows reshapes what we have at the moment, rather than representing a completely new start:

1) The House of Commons would in future have constituencies of equal size. This very basic reform has, scandalously, been blocked due to considerations of narrow party advantage. Before each election, the changes needed to retain equal size should be made.

2) The number of MPs would be reduced to 600 (from the present 650).

3) The number of constituencies would be reduced to 450.

4) Voting in the constituencies would be on a first-past-the-post system, as now.

5) 150 seats would be allocated to 'national MPs' who are not attached to a constituency. They would gain election in the order of priority on their party lists, in proportion to the votes cast for their party nationally. In other words, this element of the system would be by PR. For any party to get national MPs they must achieve at least 15 per cent of the total votes cast. In this way, the system would continue to squeeze out minority parties. Parties may choose to put their most prominent MPs on the national list to reduce the risk of losing top performers via an electoral upset. These are also the MPs often too busy to deal with constituency matters properly.

Pausing here, it can be seen that although the link between most MPs and their area remains, most votes cast in the election (other than for small parties) have an impact on the final result.

Other technical, but important, reforms would combat voting fraud. As a recent scandal in Tower Hamlets illustrated, the postal voting system is open to abuse. Care needs to be taken about the voting list and identity issues. The standard needed is the same as required for financial transactions. However, in order that voting is made easy, people should be able to qualify to vote where they live by presenting suitable identification at the polling booth, even if they have not preregistered.

The reduction in the number of MPs is not intended as an economy measure. Although MPs should not be in politics for the salary, there is scope to pay them a bit more. Thanks to repeated exercises in restraint, our prime minister now earns little more than the French President's private hairdresser. (As a by the by, raising pay might smooth the way towards acceptance of the changes.)

More radical change is needed in relation to the upper chamber. Let's get rid of Lords altogether there. Hereditary courtesy titles can remain as historic mementos, but the upper chamber is there for serious modern law making.

Here goes again …

1) The name could be changed to the 'Senate' and the members would be senators.

2) There would be 500 senators, whose appointment shadows the Commons, i.e. the composition of the Senate changes at the same time as the Commons.

3) 350 senators would be appointed by parties in the Commons in the same proportion as they are represented there. It

would, as now happens in practice, be up to the parties themselves to decide who to send to the upper chamber.

4) 150 senators with no party affiliation would be appointed for each term of the Senate (usually five years) by an appointments commission. The idea would be to replicate the present position whereby some active cross-benchers usefully contribute to the work of the house. This gives a chance to those able to contribute usefully to public life who do not want to be involved in party politics.

5) The role of the Senate would be consultative, but it would have the power to amend proposed laws once. In other words, to ask the Commons to think again. The Commons would, as the elected chamber, have the ability to overrule the Senate – if necessary, quickly.

6) The Senate would retain the ability to initiate new proposed laws. This might be a good way of getting desirable and uncontroversial legislation into law and relieve pressure on the Commons.

Although unable to block the will of the elected Commons, the Senate could be an effective and influential body. With a bit of luck, its members would be of high calibre, many of them with plenty of experience of high-level politics. The Senate's power would largely be the power of persuasion, which is not to be dismissed lightly if a point is a good one. As with the Commons, the Senate could and should use a committee structure to explore important issues of the day by summoning people to answer questions and then producing reports.

Even the current, flawed body that is the Lords does useful work in a less pressurised, more reflective way than the Commons. This could be carried over to the Senate, helped by the fact that the first Senate would presumably include many of the more effective members of the Lords. The upper house could be like a high-level, postgraduate academic institution specialising in public affairs, with the addition of a genuine ability to influence them, and 500 members should be enough to encompass a wide range of expertise but few enough for people to interact effectively.

As for the monarchy, no change would be necessary to implement the above. If it continued to work well in practice, it could keep going. Sweeping it away at the same time as these suggested reforms would also involve unnecessary distractions. Other governments would need to be involved, given the monarch's status as head of state in other countries.

Reforming Parliament should improve the law-making process. We will now consider what this can be applied to.

Making enterprise and co-operation work

State-run enterprises

Even in an enterprise economy, it is not necessary to have everything in private hands. Societies placing more emphasis on the co-operation model can decide to have some parts of it owned and run by the state. This is the concept of a 'state enterprise'.

Following the Second World War, the incoming Labour Government nationalised important parts of the economy, including utilities such as gas and electricity suppliers, the railways and the steel industry. This policy was in step with Clause 4 of the party's constitution, which provided:

> To secure for the workers by hand or by brain the full fruits of their industry and the most equitable distribution thereof that may be possible upon the basis of the common ownership of the means of production, distribution and exchange and the best obtainable system of popular administration and control of each industry or service.

The resultant experience of having 'public' (effectively civil service) control of what had previously been businesses with their own capital, managers and shareholders produced mixed results. Businesses certainly can be run this way. Coal continued to be mined, electricity fed into homes, steel was produced, and trains ran (although not up to fabled Mussolini standards of punctuality).

There was, however, a sense that something was missing. Despite the fact that money was not being siphoned off to keep shareholders happy (something disliked by critics of the enterprise model), performance was disappointing. The railways, for example, constantly required injections of public money, rather than paying money to the government from the fruits of their operation.

The nationalised industries operated from the late 1940s until many were privatised from the 1980s onwards. Critics say that they were costly, mediocre failures. Why might this come about?

Let's think about the 'enterprise' component of a state enterprise. In the case of a private one, there will be one or more people who got it going, raised the funding by satisfying shareholders and lenders that there was a good thing on offer, and then run it to try to make money and prosper. In order to stand out from the crowd (and cope with competitors), there is pressure to innovate. In order to make a profit, there is pressure to control costs carefully and be efficient.

Now, let's consider the position of someone curating the same business on behalf of the state. Firstly, he is unlikely to be a get-up-and-go entrepreneurial sort of person (entrepreneurs will want to run their own business, which gives them more control and the chance to make much more money). He or she may be hard-working and intelligent, but still a different type of economic animal – a manager, rather than an instigator.

Instead of shareholders looking over this manager's shoulder, there is the state, in the form of the relevant batch of civil servants. If more investment is needed, the state (and in due course, the taxpayer) must provide it. The state is an unusual type of shareholder; unlike private ones (and private lenders such as commercial banks), it cannot go bust. This takes some tension out of the relationship, but is that a good thing?

If entire industries are nationalised, as happened in 1945, competition ceases to be part of the equation. This is not a good thing. It takes away much of the market mechanism on which an enterprise economy relies. The associated discipline and rigour disappear. It is like a football team which never has to play a competitive match – loss of edge and effectiveness is inevitable.

The danger of a nationalised industry becoming lacklustre and inefficient is considerable. They are unlikely to be run by top industrialists. Even if they are, lack of pressure from demanding shareholders, lack of competition and the consequent lack of incentive to progress and operate economically are likely to take their toll. There are few examples of a nationalised industry coming up with an important, innovative product or service.

Let's get back on track with the railways. Although far from perfect, they are immeasurably better than they were before privatisation. Passenger numbers have soared, some profits are being made here and there and, astonishingly, some new lines and stations are being built – in contrast to the dismal history of closure, underinvestment and neglect in the nationalised era.

Society and enterprise

Nationalisation is one way of trying to give the public, as represented by the state, stakeholder involvement in a business. It cuts out the profit-seeking shareholder class. But are there other ways of getting public involvement? Yes.

When I was 9, I was trusted to buy bread from the Co-op van which visited our cul-de-sac in Newcastle. It was still warm from the bakery. I handed over the money and gave the family Co-op number (28771). In return, I was given bread, change and a small receipt with 28771 written on it. My mother collected these receipts and, when she had enough, presented them at the large city-centre Co-operative store, where they translated into fairly impressive purchasing power. This was the 'divi' (dividend), which members of the Co-operative Society like us earned. There were no external shareholders. The amount of 'divi' depended on the trading success of the Society.

In later years, the complex structure of local Co-operative societies, their principal supplier, the Co-operative Wholesale Society ('CWS'), and an involved system of governance, wilted in the face of competition from commercial grocery chains. Old-style 'divi' payments, always cumbersome to administer, disappeared to be replaced by green stamps or loyalty cards.

To its credit, the Co-op, which considers itself to be a movement, has kept going, offering a wide range of services including insurance and funerals as well as retailing. Having revived its membership arrangements, it is, via them, now paying dividends again. It also contributes to communities in which it trades. The Co-op pays a lot of attention to ethical trading standards. It is also a major supporter of the Labour Party, some of whose MPs are sponsored by it.

The Co-operative idea spread to other countries. The ethos of the movement accords with the 'co-operation' approach to politics, whereby the idea is to put community interests ahead of profit. Where there are profits, they are fed back to the members who are its main customers. There are not many examples of customer ownership elsewhere.

Another interesting idea is employee ownership. The best-known example of this in the UK is the John Lewis Partnership. Owning the John Lewis & Partners department stores, Waitrose & Partners supermarkets and other assets, this £11 billion turnover business has 84,000 people working for it. Every one of them is described as a 'partner'. All profits, after payment of salaries and other costs, are for them. There are no outside shareholders.

John Lewis is by far the largest UK business to operate like this, but there are many others. The Employee Ownership Association states that the combined turnover of its membership exceeds £30 billion each year. One pioneer of the employee ownership model is Scott Bader. Established in 1921, this chemicals company employs about 650 people and trades widely around the world. A registered charity, its constitution requires it to make significant charitable donations from its earnings.

It is disappointing that the concepts of customer and staff ownership have not made greater inroads into how enterprise works. Some innovation as to how mainstream business is structured is perhaps overdue.

Enterprise working for society

The various types of enterprise, ranging from small sole traders up to giant multinational corporations, affect owners, staff, customers and society at large. Company law covers the relationship between owners and their company and the general law is left to pick up the slack when it comes to relations between the company and its staff (via employment legislation), customers and society at large.

Britain blazed a trail in pioneering the development of the modern limited company. It is time to have a further think and come up with improvements. It should be possible to build safeguards to protect the interests of staff, customers and society into the structures of companies. If done in a way that aligns their interests, the beneficial effects could be profound. Much destructive activity (including strikes by workers) flows from a perception that they are not.

Here goes …

Current structures work quite well for smaller businesses, but they function badly in the case of the very big ones, which, because of their size (and often international reach), dominate the economy. What follows should be applicable to those:

1) Employee shareholding is desirable and should be strongly encouraged. It, more than almost anything else, serves to break down class war based on 'us and them' attitudes. It is disliked by many trade unions, who feed off this thinking, for that reason. Nonetheless, shares are routinely bestowed on senior managers because it is regarded as a good way to incentivise them. There is no reason why this should not work at all levels in a business.

2) Customer shareholding, akin to membership of a Co-operative Society, is more problematic. Many customers make only a one-off purchase, and even regular ones may not be interested. A pale shadow of the idea is to be found in various customer loyalty card arrangements, although a major objective of many of these is to sweep up data about the customer base. Nonetheless, additional benefits can be conferred. There is some mileage in mechanisms which reward loyal customers.

3) Customers are members of the public, and here it might be possible to give them a stake in the fortunes of a major business, albeit a remote one. The state runs the environment in which a business operates. Why not give it some shares?

The state as shareholder

If one accepts that it would be healthy for society to have a direct economic stake in the major businesses that dominate economic activity, thought needs to be given to how to achieve this. Conventional nationalised businesses produce uninspiring results. In a world where most big businesses have to compete internationally, they are unlikely to thrive. As state-run monopolies, they will tend to lack the flexibility and vim that success requires.

However, there are other ways of getting a slice of exciting economic action for the state, and thus society at large. State investment in private enterprise is quite common and over forty countries have sovereign wealth funds. This is particularly attractive for those currently benefitting from wasting resources, such as oil and gas. Norway, with a population of 5.4 million people, leads the way with a fund worth over US$1 trillion, a quite staggering amount. This is the world's largest.

These funds represent a store of value that a country can draw on as needed, just like any investor. Since we are talking about entire countries here, the sums involved tend to be large. Nonetheless, sovereign wealth funds are normally treated as investment vehicles, not instruments to wield political influence. Much like a pension fund, the money is spread around a number of promising-looking companies. Those managing the fund do not try to control how they operate, any more than commercial shareholders.

Past attempts at state aid for private sector businesses suggest that governments (in practice, the civil servants who work for them) are bad at picking winners in the commercial field. All too often, money has been deployed as a result of political pressure in an effort to forestall job losses in a fading business sector. Governments work better at a macro level – instead of selecting individual businesses they can encourage sectors, such as IT and professional services, not least via the education system.

The rich, it is said, are different. This certainly applies to nation states, which have one or two tricks up their sleeves that are unavailable to others. One of the most remarkable of these is an ability to conjure up new money out of thin air.

Money, as a store of value, is a confidence trick. It is valuable only for as long as the confidence remains. Recognising this, central banks in charge of the money supply operate carefully. If twice as much money is suddenly injected into the system, each unit of currency is likely to lose half of its value.

The more one considers what money really is, the more one enters an *Alice Through the Looking Glass* world. It all gets 'curiouser and curiouser'. In the right circumstances, new money can be put into the financial system without creating runaway inflation. Following the 2008 financial crisis, this is precisely what was done by major central banks, including the Bank of England. Fearful of a recession, they injected new money into the system to fuel business activity.

The golden rule is to do this only in the correct economic circumstances. These are likely to be at a time of actual, or threatened, recession. The main method of getting it into the system has been to lend it to commercial banks, enabling them, in turn, to use their commercial discretion and lend to approved customers. Some economists say that this approach is too conservative. They say that when the time has come to encourage spending, governments should spray out 'helicopter money'. In other words, give everyone some.

It is evidence of the caution brought to financial management that no government, yet, has gone for quite such a potentially popular initiative. However, money could be given to the public at one remove by putting new money into a sovereign wealth fund.

In the case of the UK, it seems strange, at first sight, to consider a sovereign wealth fund when the country has enormous, and increasing, debts. However, all sorts of people and businesses combine a mixture of debts and investments. If people only invested once they had paid off all that they owed there would be far fewer investors. The right things to think about are whether the debt burden is affordable and whether the investments are good ones. If the answer to both questions is yes, then the two can sit happily alongside each other. If the investments are good, then they can help pay off the debts in due course. The fact that you have them creates confidence on the part of those who are lending to you.

The British Government raises money by selling gilts. It pays interest on these loans and promises to repay them on a given date (the money is often raised by issuing new gilts). In contrast to a lot of other countries, the UK has never defaulted on any of these arrangements (despite distractions like world wars). At present the British Government can borrow what it needs but has to keep a careful eye on the associated cost, in the form of interest payments. This has to be met somehow – mainly from taxation.

Wait a minute. People who combine borrowing and investment can use returns from their investments to pay for the borrowing – so why can't the UK do something similar? The obvious answer is that it doesn't have a sovereign wealth fund and therefore has no offsetting investments.

This could be changed. The UK Government could provide money to a sovereign wealth fund, as an alternative to lending it to banks for them to lend it onwards. In both cases, funding is thereby injected into the world of business, but by doing it via the sovereign fund, the state is not letting go of the money. Instead, it is investing it on behalf of society.

The creation of new money, which has been pursued in slightly different forms by various financial authorities, including in the USA and the eurozone, is an effort to ensure that businesses can continue to invest and their customers have money to buy things. The inflationary effect of the new money is actually beneficial if the economy threatens to go into deflation. If that were to happen, falling prices would encourage people to hold on to their money, creating a slump in economic activity.

In the case of the UK, the extensive quantitative easing provided money for banks to lend. Borrowing this gave businesses money to work with. It would have been better if at least some of this had been in the form of new capital. Lending is often short-term and companies are cautious about becoming over-reliant on it. Capital is much more secure. Such funds are under the control of the business. At a time when the economy is looking worrying and a boost to confidence is required, the injection of new capital into the right businesses is most likely to spur them into activity, such as investing in new equipment in anticipation of better times ahead.

The City of London is one of the top two or three financial centres in the world. Finding excellent managers for the sovereign fund would not be a problem. As an investment proposition, this is much more promising than hoping that civil servants or government ministers will pick winners. Moreover, investments in commercial concerns are investments where other, experienced, investors have decided that there is money to be made.

Expert management of a sovereign fund could direct new capital, supplied by the state, to where it can do most good. It would be a win–win situation. The receiving companies benefit, and the state stands to make good investments.

However, it is important not to be flippant. There is no such thing as a free lunch and no such thing as the consequence-free creation of new money. The principle that this tends to devalue the money that already exists remains sound. This imposes limits on what is possible. However, quite a lot is. The UK's quantitative easing (money printing) in response to the financial crisis has created £435 billion of new money. Because inflation has been very low, the system was able to absorb this amount.

Imagine where we would already be if half of this had gone into a sovereign fund. Dividends from the 350 leading British companies average over 3.5 per cent a year. That would equate to an annual return for the sovereign fund of over £7.5 billion, in addition to which, as with all share investments, there would be the prospect of capital appreciation from share price increases, particularly over the long term. Over time, these could at least double the overall returns.

The entry of the state into the investment arena would not impede market dynamics. It would be just another big investment fund, alongside private ones and the sovereign wealth funds that already exist for some other countries.

It is perhaps questionable whether the 350 largest companies could have absorbed sensible injections of new capital to the tune of £217.5 billion over the years in which quantitative easing has operated. But, double this amount went somewhere into the system. Injecting funds of this magnitude into the commanding heights of the economy as capital, on behalf of society, could be a very powerful, positive dynamic.

Individuals planning for the future, including old age, are encouraged to put money away in a range of investments, in pension funds, individual savings accounts and the like.

They routinely do this while still owing money on various loans, such as mortgages, credit cards and other borrowings. It is extraordinary that the UK, as a state, does not do something similar. We happen to be the home of one of the world's top centres of excellence in the world of finance and the state is not using it.

Over time, the corporate landscape would change once society, via the state, has a stake in major businesses. It would be doing so in a very different way from the nationalisation model. Enterprises would remain commercially driven, but the state would reap the fruits of success alongside, rather than instead of, commercial investors who have decided that the businesses are a good idea. The state's share of the fruits of commercial activity would lessen the divide between the have-not 'us' and the supposedly-exploiting 'them'.

A sovereign wealth fund blends communal (co-operative) priorities with commercial nous (i.e. enterprise). As such, it doesn't really fit in with the dogmatic philosophies of either of our main parties – which is probably why this promising idea has never been tried.

Ireland is the only EU country to have a sovereign wealth fund. It has over €8 billion in it and aims, over time, to generate annual returns greater than the cost of servicing government borrowings. It is a puzzle as to why Ireland is the only EU pioneer in this area. It is possible that EU rules against certain forms of state aid act as an inhibiting factor.

Apart from actions designed to cope with the after-shocks of financial crisis, there could be other occasions when the state might acquire shareholdings in private companies. The idea is far from new – for many years, the oil giant BP was partly government owned. This is difficult territory.

Political direction risks a situation whereby politics overrides economics, leading to bad investments.

The risks would, however, be very much less if we had a professionally run sovereign fund. It would be essential for this to be shielded from political pressures. The Bank of England provides a good example. It has independent authority to set interest rates and take various other important actions in relation to the management of the economy. The sovereign fund could operate in a similar way.

Once a sovereign fund got into its stride there would be no reason to cramp its style. As with other such funds, it could choose to make some of its investments abroad. A well-run sovereign fund could be an invaluable extra, and powerful, player in the economy. When recession threatens it can assist as a channel for targeted new finance. It could help to nurture carefully selected enterprises via seed corn investments. It might even step in to rescue fundamentally sound businesses in temporary difficulty (perhaps due to rapid expansion). Like a great pension fund, it should, over time, produce good returns for the taxpayer. As such, it would be a welcome additional source of funding, entirely missing at the moment.

It would be a big and (one hopes) well-run fund. Let's be imaginative. Perhaps it could get money from sources in addition to the state.

There is another potential source of money for the fund, which to some extent represents 'society' in disguise. This is the pension industry. In the UK it invests over US$3 trillion (i.e. three times more than the immense Norwegian sovereign fund) on behalf of individuals saving for their old age. This is the second-largest pensions market in the world (just bigger than Japan's). The sums involved are so huge that the impact on the economy is considerable. As far as the pensioners are concerned, of course, the performance of pension funds is very important. Even a small percentage difference in the overall investment performance of the staggering sum of over US$3 trillion would be significant.

Those running pension investments have a demanding job. They need to be in a secure position to make payments over many years, funded by their portfolio of investments. This, coupled with the numerous regulations that govern the sector, encourages a cautious approach. One consequence is that they are major purchasers of gilts. These loans to the government help the government to pay its bills, but do not always represent profitable investments. In recent years, partly because of quantitative easing, returns have been very low.

It is the pensioners who suffer the consequences. Their spending power is reduced, which is bad for them and the economy at large. Allowing pension funds to invest some of their money in the sovereign fund, as an alternative to buying gilts, could have numerous benefits. Regulations could ensure that it was channelled in the right way. At least some of the money could be used to fund infrastructure projects, taking pressure off the government.

Remember that the government is not like the rest of us. As a last resort, it has a trump card – it can conjure up new money. This means that it could underwrite at least some of the risk faced by pension funds investing in the sovereign fund. As well as encouraging them to do so, this would enable them to be sure that they can pay pensions as required. The state would be using its guarantee power to provide security to the pension sector. Unless something went badly wrong with the infrastructure investments involved (unlikely), the guarantee would never be called upon.

Provided that the machinery enabling pension funds to take part in the sovereign fund was correctly tuned, it could represent a valuable and dynamic channel of investment. It would be a better use of some of the huge sums currently stuck in underperforming gilts. Money is most useful when it is made to work hard. The sums involved could be transformative.

A heavyweight fund could help deal with some of the failings of an earlier attempt to marry private capital with investment in public infrastructure. This is the Private Finance Initiative (PFI). The idea is not necessarily a bad one. Hospitals, bridges, roads and other assets can be funded by private investors, on terms agreed by the government. The investors receive a reliable income, but they, not the state, have to come up with the money. Additionally, they, rather than the state, often have to shoulder certain risks (such as cost overruns).

There has been an explosion of PFI projects. By 2010, they had created an obligation on the part of the government to pay more than £267 billion over time. Unfortunately, it now seems clear that the state has not always secured a good bargain and private investors have often cashed in. The taxpayer now faces many years of paying for deals that were attractive for governments at the time they were signed off but now represent a continuing burden on the public purse. PFI proved too seductive. It enabled hospitals and schools to be built without the associated cost being added to public expenditure at the time. Critics say that the resultant reduction in apparent public borrowing amounts to cooking the books.

In some cases, it is probably better for the state itself to bite the bullet and pay for the infrastructure needed for public use.

If PFI is to be used in future, greater care needs to be taken over the small print of the deals, in the light of experience. Investments in public assets via a sovereign wealth fund could be a useful part of the funding mix.

Private owners of businesses

People get rich by various means, often involving businesses. It is sometimes said that business is a game and money is the way in which you keep the score. Wealthy people are often the ones who are especially good at business. Having made their pile, they have the option of retiring, but a surprising number keep going, driving onwards into new things, because that is what they do.

Is money held by rich people useless and wasted? It is rarely static. Even if simply deposited in a bank, the process of banking means that the ability of that bank to lend increases, which may stimulate general economic activity. If the money is spent on something, even if it is an extravagant indulgence, that also stimulates activity. It takes many skilled people to build a superyacht.

Private wealth provides a pool of resource, controlled by people who often have a very good nose for business. They can and do use their money to fund enterprises, including new ones. This can be risky, but very rewarding, in every sense of the term.

Consider the position of a society without this pool of money in private hands. All investment would have to be made by the state. Civil servants would be tasked with picking the best options and state-employed managers would have the job of making things work. It is unlikely that this arrangement would work well. There are few examples of it doing so. The reason is that some people are good at some things, but not others – this also applies to institutions, such as a government.

The government operates on top of everything else. It is for government to set and apply the rules. In this way, extreme outcomes can be avoided – no more potato famines or acute deprivation. In the modern world, all sorts of rules, many of them detailed, can deal with safety and environmental issues and many other things. This is the place for the government, which decides the rules, and the civil servants and legal system, which enforce them.

To go further and have the civil servants themselves playing the game is a bit like asking Premier League referees to play high-level football matches. After all, they have to be fit and they certainly know the game, but they would perform very poorly compared to Premier League players. They are not the people for the job.

Government certainly has a big role to play in the operation of a modern economy. Fine-tuning of the rules on a regular basis may be required, but the temptation to directly enter the field of play should be resisted.

Markets

Markets enable transactions to take place between buyers and sellers. A sale is a contract. At the time it is made there must be agreement about the price and any other relevant terms. If the prospective seller seeks too high a price or unreasonable terms, then the possible customer is likely to go elsewhere, provided, that is, there are rival offerings.

The resultant competition between rival sellers creates efficiencies. Manufacturers have to drive down costs in order to sell goods at competitive prices.

Markets provide an excellent way of putting a value on goods and services. Contrast the position when the state tries to manage all aspects of the economy, as happens under communism. Even clever planners are unlikely to make accurate guesses as to the level of demand for different things or what people would be prepared to pay for them.

State planning was tried extensively in communist countries like the Soviet Union and East Germany. It was a very obvious failure, compared to the market-oriented mechanisms used in the West.

China is a very interesting example of what happens when a government seeks to run things in accordance with communist principles and what happens when, after they fail, they are abandoned. Until his death in 1976, Mao Tse Tung, the leader of the communist fight against the previous nationalist regime, ran China in accordance with his interpretation of communist doctrine. Enshrined in an iconic 'little red book', his thoughts were – and are – considered by millions to be a crucial contribution to communist thought, ranking alongside Marx, Engels and Lenin.

The introduction of communism to China was certainly disruptive and became more so in the course of various convulsions, such as the Cultural Revolution, the purpose of which was to eliminate capitalist structures and usher in a new, collectivist way of doing things. This nationwide experiment was a disaster. Tens of millions died. Mao's actions probably killed more people in the twentieth century than Stalin and Hitler combined.

Since Mao's death, China has developed a policy of 'socialism with Chinese characteristics'. This has allowed free-market commerce to thrive to such an extent that China now has more billionaires than the USA. More importantly, thanks to the adoption of market dynamics, the economy has boomed, propelling China into a position where its Gross Domestic Product (GDP) is second only to the USA and is transforming the living standards of its people for the better.

China has, within a generation, eclipsed India's economy. Ironically, this is largely because India continues to adhere to many of its old socialist practices, which inhibit development. However, India is now starting to shake itself free of some of these, and given a chance, its entrepreneurs are capable of creating world-class businesses.

China has learnt its painful lesson and is now fully committed to markets. Its present leader, Xi, looks like the most powerful since Mao. His thoughts are considered to have similar doctrinal weight. As far as markets are concerned, Xi says, 'We shall give play to the decisive role of market forces in resource allocation.'

Monopolies

For markets to work well there needs to be a real element of competition. A major problem of communism is its absence, because state-owned concerns are monopolies. However, monopolies can also emerge in a capitalist economy. A company can become so powerful that it takes over and absorbs competitors, or simply squeezes them out of the market.

On the way to becoming a monopoly, the consequences might be quite good, because in order to get to its dominant position it may have to offer excellent service and attractive prices. Once a monopoly has been achieved, however, the position is much more worrying. In the absence of competition there are fewer restraints on price rises. Even shoddy products and services may be tolerated, in the absence of alternatives (as routinely happens under communism).

The only agency powerful enough to deal with a monopoly in an important field of activity is the government. Governments can, and do, step in to prevent severe market distortions arising from monopoly, or near monopoly, power. A well-known example is the break-up of Standard Oil into no fewer than thirty-four different companies, following an anti-trust ruling (i.e. a finding of a monopoly position) in 1911. Prior to that, the company, controlled by the Rockefeller family, had owned over 90 per cent of the refined oil business in the USA.

Britain has the Competition & Markets Authority, which, among other things, considers allegations of monopoly abuses. One of the EU Commissioners covers competition. This important position has genuine teeth and the EU has not flinched from focussing attention on giant companies such as Apple and Microsoft.

Monopolies are still emerging. internet-based businesses are capable of very rapid growth, enabling the leading player to rapidly leave competitors spluttering in the dust. Thus, Google dominates the online search, Amazon leads in online retailing and Facebook and Twitter monopolise different forms of social media interaction. Other sectors are being penetrated by dominant companies, such as Airbnb (accommodation) and Uber (taxi rides), via online interactions.

Progress by this sort of enterprise can be so quick that it is hard for regulatory authorities to do much before the dominant position has been achieved. However, this still leaves governments with a range of options, all of which have problems attached.

One of these is nationalisation. It can be argued that for certain services, such as the supply of electricity or the operation of a national rail network, a state-run concern is a better form of monopoly than a commercial one seeking to extract maximum profit from its position. At least society, in the form of the state, gets the benefit of any commercial advantages derived from the monopoly position.

Another course of action is for the government to step in and engineer the structure of the market by breaking up the dominant business (as per the Standard Oil example). When former state monopolies are privatised, as was done in the UK in the case of utility companies, it is normal to create a number of private businesses, not just one, in the hope that the market mechanism will work well.

Another tool available to governments is regulation. Laws can limit how businesses operate, to the extent of constricting markets via price caps and the prevention of mergers. In the UK we have a number of regulators such as Ofwat (for water), Ofcom (communications) and Ofgem (power). They are powerful, and references to 'Ofrip' probably overstate the case …

Although the efforts of governments have some impact on monopolies, there is one feature of many of them (which also applies to giant concerns which are not monopolies) that presents huge challenges. It involves the international dimension.

Multinational businesses

The East India Company, owned by private shareholders, behaved in many ways like a country. Its turnover was bigger than many countries' entire economies and its effective power was greater than most. The progressive colonisation of the Indian subcontinent was, to a considerable extent, the work of this remarkable enterprise – something beyond the capabilities of all but the very largest countries of the time. It had tremendous geographical reach.

International entities of this kind present challenges for governments. It may be possible to make them comply with national laws in respect of product standards and such things as the terms of employment for those working within national boundaries, but what about tax?

Multinational companies can have huge turnovers and often make a great deal of money. They use national resources, such as the road network, and their employees require education, healthcare and many other expensive services. It is only fair that big, rich concerns of this kind should pay their fair share of tax – but do they?

Not usually. Those running the business want to maximise profits for their shareholders. Profit is an interesting concept. Like the nature of money, the more you look at what this means, the harder it is to define. Since tax is usually levied on profits, pinning them down and then extracting them is an important matter. If the business can arrange its affairs so that profit, when it appears, does so somewhere where it will attract little or no tax, there is a huge incentive to do so.

A huge amount of effort is put in by businesses and their advisers to minimise the tax take. With enough skill and resources, a great deal can be achieved here without breaking any laws. Multinational companies can decide where to base their various activities. They are almost invariably split into numerous different sub-entities, sometimes with complex cross-shareholdings, which can involve participation by other groups (or even governments).

Some of the locations used can be rather exotic. Brass plates – or their electronic modern equivalent – flourish on plenty of sunny little islands with convenient local laws. These places are not noted for their high tax rates or stringent regulations. Revenues and costs can be shuffled around a group, via often complex charging mechanisms.

The upshot of all this is that some of the world's very largest businesses pay remarkably little tax. Pinning down their profit is like trying to grasp a bar of soap in a world-sized bath.

This phenomenon is particularly apparent in relation to the new giants that have emerged in the internet age. As long ago as January 2015, the *Sunday Mirror* newspaper published the following estimates of UK earnings and the associated tax payments:

Company	Earnings (i.e. turnover)	UK tax paid
Apple	£6.7 billion	£12.9 million
Amazon	£4.2 billion	£4.2 million
Google	£3.3 billion	£20.4 million
Ebay	£1.3 billion	£620,000
Facebook	£371 million	£182,000

All of the above businesses, notably Facebook, will have substantially increased their turnovers since.

Trade unions

Britain was the first country to industrialise. The development of city-based factories and mills drew people from the countryside and produced concentrations of workers. This excited the interest of Marx and other thinkers. There was clearly tension between them and the factory-owning elite. Their interests were in many ways opposed: the lower the wages, the higher the profits.

Skilled workers had combined and co-operated for centuries, forming guilds which, among other things, often provided procedures for regulating training and admission. Many of these ancient institutions live on as City of London livery companies, having long ago turned themselves largely into upmarket dining clubs.

Those following a skilled trade were often capable of securing a reasonable living without creating disturbances or demonstrations and their guilds were not regarded as threatening – however, combinations of hundreds, or thousands, of unskilled workers were. Fearful of the implications, successive governments resisted the emergence of the new 'trade unions' and their worrying ability to cause disruption, notably by strikes.

It was not possible to keep the cork in the bottle. By the early twentieth century, unions had emerged as a major force in society. Strike action became legal and even unskilled workers, by combining in a union, were able to exercise considerable bargaining power.

In Britain, the story of the twentieth century is in large part the story of the rise, and (to some extent) later fall, of the mass union movement and its influence. The Labour Party sprang from this and is still closely allied to it. Trade unions were impossible to ignore.

The incoming Labour Government in 1945 introduced transformative change, establishing post-war contours that are still in evidence today. Some say that the 1940s count as Britain's greatest decade: helping to turn back tyranny against the odds by fighting in the war and then planting the roots of the welfare state as soon as it was finished.

By the 1950s the West German economic miracle was under way, as a disgraced country rapidly converted itself into a prosperous modern state. Meanwhile, the British economy ambled forwards. Living standards improved. Harold Macmillan, the Conservative Prime Minister, told us 'you've never had it so good' in 1957.

Even if that was right, all was not well. There was a damaging self-reinforcing mix of old-fashioned, mediocre managements, underinvestment in research, machinery and training, and militant and obstructive trade unionism. While the West German industrial machine purred away (equipped with its new factories), a complacent Britain found itself overtaken.

In the 1960s and 1970s one of the busiest reporters on BBC News was the 'industrial correspondent'. His task (they were all men, in those days) was to report on the latest major strike. Talking over TV images of pickets huddled round braziers at the factory gates, he would give an account of the gap between the wage demands and the employer's offer, the lost production and the possibility of a meeting in 10 Downing Street over tea and sandwiches in an effort to resolve matters. Grim-faced union bosses said things like, 'My members are 100 per cent solid.' Unions were very powerful. The hit song 'I'm a union man' by the Strawbs captured things perfectly in 1973 – 'You don't get me, I'm part of the union ...'.

It was clear that not all strikes were just about pay. There was an obvious political edge to some of them. The 1973 strike by coal miners (in the days when coal production was still of crucial importance) brought down Edward Heath's Conservative Government early in 1974. The country had faced regular power cuts (I remember working with an oil lamp on my office desk). Heath called an election, largely on the issue of whether the unions or the government should run things. He was voted out.

This was the background to the biggest and most significant strike action since the Second World War. Lasting about a year until the miners accepted defeat in 1985, it represented a struggle between a very militant leader of the National Union of Mineworkers (Arthur Scargill) and a determined prime minister (Margaret Thatcher). Due in part to tactical errors and overreaching, Scargill failed to get generalised support from other unions, or even the support of all miners.

Always regarded as 'the shock troops of the labour movement', the defeated miners never again attempted a similar challenge. Partly for environmental reasons, their industry has now disappeared, and trade unionism has entered a new age.

Mining is not the only industry to have seen a massive reduction in its workforce, with its inevitable shrinkage in union membership. There were 13 million British trade union members in 1979. By 2012, the total was about 6 million, although unions remain strong in the public sector and in some parts of the economy that have been state run in the past, such as the railways. It is notable that the railways are, at present, strike prone – something of an echo of the 1970s.

The public sector still provides large concentrations of workers where trade unions can function on traditional lines. Part of the intense nervousness about any private sector involvement in the National Health Service (NHS) is probably driven by a desire not to dilute this. The 'labour movement' relies on the unions. It does not want them weakened further.

Some would like to see extensive renationalisation, attendant re-expansion of union membership and the restoration of union bosses to the position of prominence that they enjoyed in the 1970s. Some would be alarmed at such developments. Unions have in the past been routinely conservative (with a small 'c'). Their desire to protect members and their jobs has led them repeatedly to resist most forms of change. (That is what is currently happening as rail companies try to introduce driver-only trains.) This can be dangerous to the health of any enterprise in today's fast-moving world.

However, rather than try to cling on to a twentieth-century model, trade unions could adapt. Members of today's fragmented, mobile workforce still need representation in a world where employers hold most of the bargaining chips. A clue to the way forwards lies in the word 'trade'. Just as the old guilds assisted those involved in their respective occupations, so unions can help individuals with their careers in a chosen sector.

In return for membership fees, a whole range of services and advice can be made available, in a modern way, taking advantage, where appropriate, of online resources like links to advice videos. Telephone or video consultations with a union expert when considering the terms of a new contract, or when a disciplinary issue arises, could be very valuable. Unions could take the bull by the horns and offer job-finding services, marrying applicants to those seeking staff (and charging the employer a fee).

Most radically of all, unions with large numbers of members working for a business could invest in that business. What a turnaround that would be! Traditionally, the employer, as 'the other side', was invariably viewed as the opponent. All too often this was via short-term, zero-sum thinking, whereby anything beneficial to the employer was viewed as occurring at a cost to the workers. But what is so wrong about working on the same side? Why will that be prejudicial to the members, if the company thrives and expands?

Having some sort of presence on the employers' side of the fence is routine in Germany, whose post-war labour relations have consistently been much better than the UK's. There is worker representation at board level and a general, but invaluable, recognition that it is in the interests of everyone for the business to succeed.

Modern unions have an important and useful role to play. Workers need advice and protection, even if this rarely requires the draconian and damaging step of a strike. Experienced union negotiators can help to shape employment practices. In the interests of their members, they need to think modern and think ahead. They need a deep, not superficial, understanding of their industry and the businesses working within it. Like the old guilds, they could play an important role in promoting a sector, taking a close interest in training and the maintenance of standards. They need to be 'trade' unions.

A modernised approach to work

Where are jobs going to come from?

At present, to the astonishment of many, UK employment levels are high. There are, nonetheless, considerable concerns. Real wages seem stuck. Many of the jobs recently created are low paid. Technology advances apace and automation and computerisation threaten to eliminate many traditional occupations.

This is not a new worry. Every improvement in the means of production has led to concerns of this kind. They are by no means fanciful. Jobs do disappear. The upside is that new ones emerge. A generation ago, almost nobody was a website designer.

Some things are very hard, if not impossible, to automate. Driverless vehicles are planned, but for the foreseeable future the logistics industry will still need a lot of people, and there is a shortage of HGV drivers at present. The large and growing catering, hospitality and tourism industry is very labour intensive. There is also a big shortage of responsible carers for the elderly. Modern society is crucially dependent on high education and skill levels. Providing the required teachers of these is another obvious growth area.

Fewer people are going to be needed to do the grunt work of making things, just as agriculture (once a huge employer) now gets by with very few workers, thanks to mechanisation. The new jobs are often going to be in the activities which require human interaction. By definition, machines are not equipped to do that. Most modern economies, particularly Britain's, are heavily focussed on the service sector. This is likely to continue to thrive. Professional services like law and accountancy are much bigger chunks of the economy than is generally supposed. A significant part of the income that they generate comes from abroad.

Crowded Britain is crying out for all manner of infrastructure improvements. Houses, hospitals, schools, rail links – even unfashionable but useful roads – all need to be built. We need faster, more reliable broadband and better mobile phone connections.

And let's not forget the creative industries. Thanks to the use of English, they tend to be world-beaters.

All of the above areas offer the prospect of new jobs.

Incubator businesses

Employment is stimulated by the creation of new businesses. As they grow, they tend to take on more people. In contrast, big businesses with plenty of staff often reduce their head count over time, as new ways of doing things are adopted, technology has its effect and cost-cutting managements seek to reduce all forms of expenditure, including wages.

New businesses need to be nurtured. They are a good source of innovation as well as employment and some of them will grow into the major players of the future. Like all things in their infancy, a new concern can be frail and vulnerable. Raising money can be a problem. The founders may not have much, and there are considerable difficulties in getting external shareholder investments in start-ups while banks are reluctant to lend to an untested new outfit.

Someone starting a business is usually good at something, which acts as the driver. But one person is unlikely to have all of the skills that a well-run business needs. A caterer may not be very good at accounts, or contracts, for example.

One of the hardest things for a business to do is migrate from a one-person enterprise to one with two people in it. This is a major step – a 100 per cent increase in head count. It carries with it a whole host of obligations, including detailed provisions covering employment. Many talented one-person businesses stay that way because the challenges are so off-putting.

This is very unfortunate. It deprives people of the opportunity to work alongside someone with the get-up-and-go needed to set up as a plumber, wedding dress maker, or whatever – someone who is able to pass on useful skills at close quarters. Depressingly few plumbers now want to take on apprentices. As a result, the average age of UK plumbers is getting worryingly high.

There should be much better mechanisms for helping those who are setting out on their own in business. They should be able to concentrate on what they do well and rely on affordable support for all of the 'back office' functions.

Since we are concerned with rearing businesses here, the most effective support is likely to come from other businesses, rather than government institutions. There is a big, and largely unexploited, opening for commercial providers of the sort of support that young businesses need. Like all good business arrangements, they should be win–win. In other words, both sides benefit.

Let us suppose that some offices, or perhaps old classrooms in a former school, are unoccupied. The support provider could rent them, probably at low cost, and offer desks, plus some basic facilities, for rent by the month. There would, no doubt, be internet and landline connections, refreshment facilities, shared copying and printing machines, and perhaps a bookable meeting room.

Every desk might be used by a different business, each of which now has the anchor of a base from which to operate. Not everyone has a home that is suitable for this and operating on your own from home can be a lonely process. Most people thrive on the buzz of being surrounded by others at work. All the more so if they are kindred spirits – in this case, people with the confidence and skills to set up on their own.

The support provider business could, in return for the appropriate payments, make life easier for the emergent businesses in many other ways. It could operate as the registered office for those that are companies. It could offer shared support in the form of a telephone answering service and perhaps the issue and collection of invoices.

There are few barriers to the establishment of incubator centres of this kind. They could, and should, be hives of activity and rapidly become an important component of the economy. They would offer a pathway into business for those emerging from the education system and those returning to it after time spent caring for children or setting up something after having lost employment.

Incubator centres could also take advantage of mentoring by retired – and perhaps successful – people with time to spare, who are happy to get involved. In this way, they could harness the (at present, largely wasted) power of the numerous experienced individuals in this position.

There are probably hundreds of thousands of these. Not all will be interested, and many will only be looking for part-time involvement. Nonetheless, the contributions available could be very useful. As people progress in their careers they often rise in an organisation. Higher levels often have fewer people than the ranks lower down. In time, there can be pressure on still-capable individuals to make way for those thrusting their way up from below. Out they go – and what then? By harnessing their talents via their inputs into incubator centres, they could offer a wide range of skilled support, and possibly sometimes investment, which would turbo charge the progress of the new businesses.

Business often benefits from networking and sharing ideas. There can be a serendipity factor at work, as sometimes surprising connections are made. Incubator centres, particularly if assisted by the right mentoring in the form of 'grey power', should offer plenty of fertile possibilities.

The private sector needs people with the right skills. Big business can, of course, choose to get involved. In our part of the world, Dyson is leading the way by doing nothing less than establishing its own education facility. In due course, degrees will be awarded to graduates of this imaginative place of learning. It is based in Dyson's new research centre on a former military airfield. There are many ways in which talent can be nurtured. The Dyson initiative highlights what can be achieved by closely linking the worlds of business and education. Dyson is incubating its future workforce.

So, unless we lose our mojo as a country, there should be jobs to do. What should a modern one look like?

The F-word ... 'flexibility'

Someone entering the world of work now should plan to be adaptable. It is likely to change greatly in a working life of forty years or more. Some giant employers remain, such as the National Health Service, educational institutions and other branches of the public sector. Even in those, however, the need to accept change and to constantly refresh skills is likely to be acute.

In the business world, lifelong employment with one employer is likely to be the exception rather than the rule. Economic forces require businesses themselves to rapidly adapt or die. In the process, jobs can disappear or be changed beyond recognition. Thanks to computerisation, bookkeeping procedures were transformed within a generation. There are many other examples.

The law has stepped in to try to protect people from the harshest consequences of change in the field of employment. The government often gets involved if a major business is about to shed a lot of staff. But there are obvious limits to what can be done. Once the economic foundation for a job goes, it is time for the employee to move on.

In a fast-changing world where much of the old stability has gone, there is a need for new thinking about how people should approach work and its relationship with everything else that they want to do in life. In the past, life has typically been lived in rather rigid segments, following a sequence of education, work (often combined with parenthood and/or care for elderly relatives) and retirement (often involving care for grandchildren). Sport, holidays and leisure might be fitted in as well, together with dealing with unwelcome things like illness and injury.

The rapid pace of change will lead to a requirement for much more flexibility. Few will be able to sail through a career solely on the strength of what they learnt in their youth. There will be a pressing requirement to retrain, adapt and keep up to date. The education phase of life can, and should, be lifelong.

Flexibility will not just involve a willingness to change employers (who will come and go, expand and shrink, in response to economic pressures). There will often be a need to change careers. The old convention of having one job might wither. What is so sacrosanct about it? From the workers' point of view, it means that all their eggs are in one basket. If they have two, three or more jobs, they are more secure. Why not drive a tube train for a couple of hours during the morning rush hour, spend the rest of the day at home, and work in a restaurant three evenings a week? From the employer's perspective, it will often be attractive to have workers available at peak times, without committing to a large workforce of full-timers.

Many people are now subject to zero-hours contracts (which give no guarantee of any work at all) or have opted to be self-employed, in what is sometimes called 'the gig economy'. The boundaries between employment and self-employment are far from clear cut. Some people, including those providing professional or consultancy services, obviously function as self-contained, one-person businesses, with a range of customers or clients. The position of Uber taxi drivers, or Deliveroo cyclists, however, is more questionable. Since all of the work is assigned by one entity, which also dictates the terms of operation, to what extent are they self-employed? Critics say that all that is happening is that the big operator (such as Uber) is dodging the costs and responsibilities that the law places on employers. Nonetheless, it is clear that many of those driving for Uber like the position that they are in, welcome the marketing and other support provided, and enjoy the opportunity to decide when to work.

The law should not be heavy-footed to the extent of squashing new models of work on dogmatic grounds. Nor should government abandon its important 'refereeing' role. There should be space for a legal third way, between clear, independent self-employment and the full majesty of our rather detailed employment laws. Abuses would be stopped. Those choosing to work in the gig economy would trade some of the benefits of formal employment for the greater flexibility that many of them want.

A move away from the 'one full-time job' model would also help people to pace their lives to deal with the demands of childcare, or care of the elderly and disabled. It is ridiculous, for instance, to lose the services of trained nurses due to a reluctance to countenance short-time working, or regular hours. More generally, it is important that parents taking time to look after children have an opportunity to stay in the swim by doing some work, making a return to a more full-time regime later very much easier.

If there is flexibility in the system, leaving a particular job will lose much of its terror. You may have more than one at a time. With non-rigid employment structures there should be more work options.

Pensions and the 'third age'

Many seek the rewards of a successful career and are prepared to make sacrifices, such as working long hours, in order to achieve these. For some, transition to retirement can be a damaging shock. Jobs are considered to be an indicator of status. People can have a sense, which may be unconscious, that 'they are what they do'. Once the anchor of a job disappears, they feel rudderless and disorientated.

They may also feel poor. One of the drivers towards making money via work is to be able to have a prosperous retirement. Outside the public sector, work-based pensions have effectively shrunk in recent years. This is for several reasons. The biggest one is increased life expectancy. A pension fund that is adequate to provide for ten years becomes stressed if the pensioner lives for twenty-five. Under-provision for retirement, coupled with longer lifespans, represents a ticking economic time bomb of alarming proportions.

It is also a good news story in disguise. That is, provided we change our approach to the work–life cycle. The state pension kicks in at the age of 65, at which point people are labelled 'old-age pensioners' and are regarded as a dependent drag on society. Some people are, especially in advanced old age.

We all run out of road eventually, but for many of us this certainly doesn't happen at 65. 'Third agers' are a hugely underused resource. This comes about because of pessimistic traditional perceptions of what the elderly can do and of the continuing notion that work is a full-time commitment.

The millions of third agers, between them, represent a huge pool of experienced potential workers. Not all of them want work, but many do, for reasons of economics, boredom or simply a continuing desire to be involved in things and do stuff.

As with so much to do with work, it is important to focus on the F-word – 'flexibility'. As far as is necessary, the law needs to loosen up to encourage it. The older one gets, the more limitations there are on what can be done. Employers should not have to risk being stuck with any kind of incapable worker, including those who have become 'past it'. This is not age discrimination, it is capability discrimination.

A modern approach to work will recognise that people have varying wants and needs, and that these change over time. Getting work will be essential for most, but it should not have to be a constant full-time slog. If there is confidence that some work is likely after what is now considered to be 'retirement age', much pressure can be lifted. Work can be reduced, or stopped, in mid-career, for example when children are young. Income will suffer at the time, but pension pots will not have to be so big – because people will typically work, often part-time, well into the third age.

Life is there to be enjoyed. Not everyone wants to burn up their middle years by incessant work and then twiddle their thumbs for over twenty years in retirement …

Summary

Solutions are to be found via the following:

1) A 'demos' is needed. Society needs sufficient cohesion to work properly, which requires communication and a tolerance of difference combined with effective legal and social mechanisms.

2) The common law is a tried, tested and valuable part of the mix.

3) A new, less two-dimensional and compartmentalised approach to politics is needed.

4) Democracy needs to be protected by paying attention to how Parliament works. Here major changes are needed.

5) Economics is central to how society works (Marx certainly got this bit right). It is important to align the separate, but not necessarily opposing, interests of the

four stakeholder groups: owners, workers, customers and society. Over time, new business structures can be evolved to help achieve this.

6) A sovereign wealth fund could be a powerful agency, giving society a worthwhile stake in the commanding heights of the economy without the drawbacks of nationalisation. Independent, like the Bank of England, and skilfully managed, it could direct investments where they will be most effective and, among other things, help to stave off recessionary pressures.

7) The immense sums curated by the UK pensions industry could be better deployed, particularly via a carefully structured relationship with the sovereign wealth fund.

8) It should be recognised that wealthy private individuals play an important part in the economy. (See also the next part of this book.)

9) Markets provide a vital dynamic. Part of the state's role is to referee them. The state has a key role in establishing the rules within which enterprises must operate and then enforcing them.

10) The state should set the rules and monitor performance against them. It should not try to play the game itself via nationalisation.

11) Monopolies are undesirable, but if they are unavoidable in a sector then it is better for them to be state owned than

private. Private monopolies do not confer the economic benefits that other enterprises do, because of the lack of the discipline generated by markets.

12) Multinational enterprises require special attention due to the monopoly risk and difficulty in collecting tax from them.

13) Much can be done to incubate new businesses.

14) People over 65 are a valuable and very underused resource.

15) We need a much more flexible approach to patterns of work.

We will now look at how these ideas come into play in relation to major areas that the government has to deal with. We start by looking after the money.

3

KEY GOVERNMENT FUNCTIONS

Managing the economy: wealth and tax

Should we tolerate the rich?

Most people would benefit in all sorts of ways if they had more money. Very good reasons are needed to tolerate a situation where, despite this, a small number have far more money than could ever produce practical benefits for them. As someone gets richer, the additional benefits from getting better off become more and more marginal:

Alf, with nothing at all, has his situation dramatically improved if he is given £10. This will pay for a meal, or possibly somewhere very basic to sleep – probably in some kind of shared dormitory.

£100 produces a big improvement for Brenda, who can feed herself for a day and pay for somewhere to sleep in moderate comfort.

£1,000 for Clive means that he can do all this for at least a week and still have money for other things, such as travel and making calls in an effort to find work.

£10,000 for Diane gives her plenty of scope to take decisions about her lifestyle. There is no room for extravagance but finding a deposit for somewhere to rent and call home is not a problem. She also can look around for work and need not take the first thing that comes along. Even a holiday might be managed, along with some other leisure time. She is in a position to operate in the mainstream of society and economic life.

£100,000 for Edward may enable him to be a house owner if he gets a reasonably well-rewarded job.

£1 million for Faye makes her much better off than most. Depending on her age, family commitments and aspirations, however, she may well want to work to sustain her lifestyle.

£10 million for George makes work optional. If he so chooses, he can be a member of the leisured classes, with considerable scope to do what he wants.

£100 million for Hannah leaves her just outside the *Sunday Times* rich list of the 1,000 most wealthy people in the UK. Her money alone makes her something of a known figure, regardless of whatever else she does. At this level, she almost certainly has some staff, more than one comfortable home and several vehicles. Security becomes a concern, especially in relation to any children and the associated kidnap risk. However nice and approachable Hannah is, it is very difficult to live like a normal person. In all sorts of ways, the money is a barrier.

£1 billion for Ian makes him one of the richest 200 people in the UK. Anything that money can buy to make his life comfortable, including his own jet, can easily be afforded. A surprising amount of Ian's time will be absorbed by managing what he owns, which probably includes at least one substantial business.

£10 billion makes Julia one of the world's richest people. She is so wealthy that it might be sensible to buy a Premiership football team, if she is interested in the game. There are people with much more money than Julia.

Are we comfortable with these different levels of wealth? If not, what should be done about it? If some levelling process is to be applied, what is the datum line to be? Achieving equality is likely to be impossible. Do we accept a variation that seeks to make sure that everyone is at least as well off as Diane (£10,000) but no one is allowed to be better off than Faye (£1 million)? How could this possibly be achieved in practice?

There is an important philosophical difference between the enterprise and co-operative (or collective) political visions. The enterprise camp considers individual property rights to be of central importance. Taxation by the state is acceptable but should not be at confiscatory levels and the core ownership of wealth is held by individuals, not the state.

The collective approach considers core ownership to be held by the state. It then allows individuals to hold and use assets, at its discretion. This may sound Marxist and has an important echo in the wording of the Labour Party's now discontinued Clause 4. However, the concept pre-dates Marx by hundreds of years. In Britain, major assets, primarily land, belonged to the Crown. For a long time, this was personified by the monarch, who bestowed estates on the aristocrats who ran much of the country. Sometimes the king's power was also used to remove them.

Even today English land law, the main elements of which were cut and dried by 1189, maintains the concept that all land, even 'freehold', is held subject to the Crown (i.e. the state). If land, or some other asset, has no owner then it passes to the state. This can arise if someone dies without any will or relatives to inherit. The principle also applies to discoveries of buried treasure.

So, why should we have the right to decide how much wealth someone should have?

Many people will answer that question by saying that big discrepancies in wealth are unfair. They can then go on to say that society, through the agencies of government, can and should undertake some redistribution, to reduce, or eliminate, the differences.

We have already seen that the experiment of communism, which in theory espoused this levelling-down idea, failed. For all sorts of reasons, complete levelling is very difficult to achieve. And even if it could be, would that be fair? Some people are bright, energetic, innovative, hard-working and, for these reasons, successful. They are often society's innovators and employers. Others, whether talented or not, choose to sit around doing little or nothing. Is it fair that all these people should get the same rewards?

Almost all societies, including the UK, take 'levelling' steps. This is done via taxation, to take money away, and welfare payments, to give it to others. In the UK, the sums involved are considerable. Despite these redistributive efforts, we still have some very rich and some much less well-off individuals. Much political debate deals with the issue of whether the current balance is the right one.

Tax

In the UK, the amount of income tax paid by higher earners as a proportion of the total has increased progressively. Based on 2017 figures supplied by Her Majesty's Revenue and Customs

(HMRC) the top 1 per cent, earning more than £162,000 per annum, paid about 27 per cent of the total. The top 10 per cent (earning over £51,400 per annum) paid nearly 60 per cent.

Wealthy as some people are, care needs to be taken when dealing with the large numbers involved in the relevant calculations. When even a large sum is spread between tens of millions of people it amounts to not very much each. And there are other practical considerations. Someone who is happy to live here and pay, say, 40 per cent tax may not be happy to do so if the rate goes up to 60 per cent or more. High earners are often capable people and are therefore sought after elsewhere. They might move away. Lower taxes, on the other hand, can attract people. London has more French workers than all but five French cities, largely because of the lower rates for high earners that apply in the UK.

Thought needs to be given to the purpose of taxation. Is it to level down wealth, in the pursuit of fairness? Is it to raise money for the numerous things that governments spend it on? Or is it a bit of both?

It is argued that there is a sweet spot if the aim is to maximise government tax revenue. The Laffer curve is a projection of the anticipated tax take at different rates of tax. If the tax rate is zero, then there is no revenue. If it is 100 per cent, there is almost certainly no revenue, since the activity being taxed (work, for example) would not be worthwhile. As tax rates increase, so does revenue, up to a certain point where resistance kicks in (i.e. people do less work). Revenue then declines at an increasing rate, relative to increasing tax rates.

Reference is made to this fairly simple concept when decisions are made as to which tax rates to apply. The UK Institute for Fiscal Studies (an independent body) did this when income tax rates were reduced from 50 per cent to 45 per cent for high earners. It thought that the reduction in tax receipts would be relatively low. In other words, the fact that people would retain more of their earnings would cause them to increase them, paying tax on the higher earnings at the lower rate sufficient to make up much of the theoretical shortfall.

However, not everyone is convinced by the Laffer curve concept. Many think that raising rates of tax will always increase revenue. This places faith in the idea that, even if the rates are raised high, the revenue-earning activity will continue at the same level.

Effective taxation has been described as like plucking the maximum number of feathers from a goose with the minimum of clucks. Laffer curve considerations come into play. Another thought is that the goose needs to be kept healthy – killing the one that lays the golden eggs is particularly stupid.

Since the government is the 'they', as in 'they ought to do something about it', pressure on its finances is relentless. In order to try to pluck the goose effectively, there are taxes all over the place. Some of the complications flow from efforts to fine-tune the way the economy works (e.g. by taxing polluting activity highly).

The product of many years of taxation development is an immense thicket of law and regulation. A whole army of accountants, lawyers and financial advisers makes a fat living grappling with it all. Every regulation and exception creates boundaries and cracks, often exploited unexpectedly for tax avoidance, on the 'where there's a law, there's a flaw' principle.

One thing that is not happening is any pursuit of the 'keep it simple' principle. Matters would be considerably improved if a government of vision came to power after saying something like this to the electorate:

> The present system is far too complicated. We are going to simplify it dramatically. There will be winners and losers as we do so and the transition to the new arrangements will be a bit of a bumpy ride. However, we are clear about where we are going with our changes and once they have bedded in things will be very much better, because everything will be much clearer and simpler than at present. Partly because of this, it will be much easier to make sure that those with a relevant level of earnings pay the proper amount of tax.

These are the key principles that we will follow:

1. The total effect of the changes overall will be revenue neutral for the first two years. In other words, the government will set taxes at levels which preserve its revenues. This will help to minimise disruption.

2. People who work deserve to be rewarded. Welfare payments will be adequate, but low. However, the present practice is that benefit is rapidly withdrawn if someone starts to earn. This means that some of the poorest in society are paying the highest marginal rates of tax (over 60 per cent) as benefits are withdrawn as they find work. This will stop. No one earning less than the income attracting the higher tax band will pay an effective rate of tax above the basic rate. This will, initially, be very costly to achieve. In the medium term, this change will

greatly encourage the long-term unemployed to enter the workforce. The cost of this change should then be met by reductions in the welfare budget, as pay replaces benefits.

3. Some people are unable to manage their finances, leading to non-payment of rent and possible eviction. Welfare benefits will be paid directly to landlords in such cases. In extreme cases, food vouchers, rather than cash, will be dispensed.

4. National Insurance (NI) contributions have effectively been a tax on the working population and their employers. There is no resultant fund. Pensions and other benefits are paid for via general taxation. These contributions will stop.

5. Retired people do not pay NI contributions. They will get a higher personal allowance for income tax purposes to compensate them for the fact that the burden formerly borne by NI will in future be paid from general taxation. However, well-off retired people have in many ways had a generational dividend and the allowance level set will mean that they will, if they are high earners, be paying more than hitherto.

6. The recent practice of raising the point at which people start to pay tax will continue, so that those with modest incomes, including pensions, will pay none.

7. There will be a basic rate of income tax and a higher rate on income above a certain figure.

8. The higher rate will not exceed 40 per cent. Anything above this starts to look confiscatory. However, this rate should be paid. All of the complex structure of allowances which enable it to be avoided will be swept away.

9. The same process of simplification will apply to companies. There will be two rates of tax, the higher, as with income tax, applying to the bigger earners. Associated businesses will count as one earner. As with income tax, the present complex system of reliefs, which reduces the tax take, will be abolished.

10. Tax on companies currently applies to profits. Here there will be a change, introducing a new level of complication. Profits will be calculated, as they are now, but a new system will apply to the larger businesses, including multinational ones, which have profits, or turnovers, above certain levels. Big businesses of this kind can deal with complexity. They are also the concerns that can structure their operations in such a way that profits are declared primarily in another jurisdiction, with lower tax rates. For this category of large businesses, tax will be levied on a combination of profit and the turnover achieved from trading in the UK.

11. Inheritance tax will continue as at present, with a rate of 40 per cent.

12. So far as VAT (an expenditure tax) is concerned, essential items, such as tampons, will cease to be taxed. Generally, expenditure taxes will be higher on luxury items.

13. There will be no wealth or mansion tax. This would be an intrusive new form of taxation which would be difficult to administer well. However, the current system of real estate taxation in the form of rates is well overdue for review, based as it is on a very artificial and out-of-date valuation model. There will be a re-rating exercise. The challenges of this must not be underestimated. It requires something like the creation of a modern Domesday Book. However, modern technology can be brought to bear. Via computer imagery, including satellite, property can be recorded in detail and those details then kept up to date. Much of the process of inputting will be done by the owners themselves.

14. So far as residences are concerned, there will be higher upper tiers than at present, ensuring that very valuable ones pay at much higher levels. It is particularly important to get revenue in respect of empty luxury premises.

15. Business rates will be kept to relatively modest levels. At present, the system penalises those businesses that, for one reason or another, require expensive – and often extensive – properties. This is not the right approach. It should be the businesses that are making the most money who contribute the most via the taxation system. They may require little (or if abroad, no) UK real estate from which to operate. Note that a more restrained approach to business rates will help to avoid the hollowing out of town centres and the closure of community-focussed enterprises such as local shops and pubs.

16. Customs duties will be collected with reference to a computerised system of tracking goods, using barcodes, blockchain technologies and online payments. This will reduce the need for physical inspections and free up Customs and Excise staff to conduct investigations and tackle fraud. The modern systems will facilitate international trade, which we are keen to encourage.

17. We will continue to press for tariff-free trade across international boundaries.

The new taxation landscape will squeeze out a lot of cost associated with the operation of the current, densely complex, system. It will enable all taxpayers, commercial and private, to easily plan their affairs. It will eliminate long-standing distortions in the allocation of resources. It gives a strong helping hand to those at the bottom of the earnings ladder and encourages those currently on welfare to join it. The better off will be required to contribute substantial proportions of their earnings, without the wriggle room that they have enjoyed up to now. But this government recognises their contribution, and this will not be at confiscatory levels. Multinational concerns deriving large revenues from us will, in future, pay tax on them.

Trade

Trade is vital to the economy. It is dependent on international relationships. We will come to it later in the book.

Welfare

If you want to see where the government's money goes, welfare spending is a good place to start. Welfare includes state pensions, money spent on care for the elderly, ill or disabled, and income and other forms of support for the poor or unemployed. For 2017, the total cost is expected to have been about £264 billion, representing 34 per cent of total government expenditure. This is the biggest call on the public purse.

Pensions account for over 40 per cent of welfare spending and this is likely to increase as more people reach pensionable age and life expectancy keeps rising.

The huge sums involved represent an apparently attractive target for a government looking for economies. One obvious move is to increase the pension age and some steps have already been taken in this direction. We can expect more.

Elsewhere in the welfare budget, reductions in expenditure seem to require difficult choices, involving what are perceived to be attacks on the most vulnerable people in society. Opinions sharply differ as to whether or not there is a major problem with an 'underclass'. Supposed characteristics of this group are a lack of work, generation after generation, total reliance on state support, large families, unhealthy lifestyles putting pressure on the health services, poor educational attainment verging on illiteracy, delinquency and antisocial behaviour.

There are, no doubt, people who tick some or all of these boxes. Such individuals undoubtedly represent a considerable cost to society, in financial and, probably, other ways.

The poor, it is said, will always be with us. The modern definition of 'relative poverty' is less than 60 per cent of median income. 'Median' is the point at which 50 per cent have a higher income and 50 per cent a lower one. Note that this income level is not the same as 'average income'. In the UK, someone at the relative poverty threshold is much better off than the shoeless, near starving conditions that were associated with 'absolute poverty' in the past. This provides little comfort. Being stuck at the bottom of the ladder of prosperity in a society has all sorts of negative consequences. There is exclusion from many of the things regarded as normal activities.

People are all different. Some who qualify for benefits do not claim them, out of pride, or sometimes ignorance. Others play the system – having children can increase family income levels and improve the prospects of securing scarce social housing, while relieving pressure to seek work.

Poverty can have a large number of causes. Unless the economy is unusually buoyant, there will always be some people who want to work and cannot find jobs. Mental illness, physical disability and drug addiction all present barriers to employment. Some people try to make a go of business and fail, going bankrupt in the process. Some people, even high earners, gamble everything away.

The underlying problems are considerable and successive governments have found them difficult to grapple with. Even the enormous sums devoted to welfare spending seem inadequate and there are constant calls for more.

These days, the state gets very involved, via a large number of agencies, to try to provide a safety net (so that no one starves or has to live on the street) and a ladder or helping hand up for those able and willing to take advantage of it.

There is resentment among many who are making a real effort if others seem to enjoy benefits (such as a house for their five children) without apparently doing anything for themselves. Other critics of the system point out that a very large number of jobs are currently being done by people from abroad, notably the eastern countries of the EU, who have taken up a large proportion of the extra jobs created by the British economy in recent years. This sits uncomfortably alongside the still very large total of UK nationals receiving welfare benefits.

The welfare system can never be perfect. Some improvements may nonetheless be found via the following:

1) At present, the system whereby benefits are withdrawn as someone finds work often results in an effective tax rate in excess of 60 per cent. This is very unfair to some of the most disadvantaged in society.

2) Recent increases in the level at which tax starts to be paid have nibbled away at the problem. No one who has crossed that threshold, due to benefit income plus earnings, should have a tax rate of more than the basic rate of tax – 'tax rate' being the combined effect of the tax and the withdrawal of benefit.

3) Benefits should be adequate for basic needs, but no more.

4) Part-time work as well as full-time work should be encouraged.

5) The national minimum wage needs to be set high enough to prevent exploitation and not so high as to choke off job creation.

6) Childcare provision is an important part of the mix ...

7) ... as is the education system, notably for adults.

8) The health service has a big role to play. Mental health, in particular, needs to be thought about. Many of the long-term unemployed are likely to be depressed.

9) Generally, the system needs to be kind but firm. Having successive generations of welfare dependency – which does occur – is corrosive for all concerned and unacceptable.

10) Achieving progress may require an expenditure surge, because the cost of removing the hugely unhelpful high tax rate as someone starts to move off benefits is likely to

be high. However, the benefits should come through quite quickly if it results in a sea change in people's behaviour. At present, many are put in a position where it makes no sense to work – which makes no sense.

More generally, poverty arises from a complex set of causes and its reduction requires a complex set of measures. The better and more prosperous the society, the more likely they are to succeed.

Care

One of the major demands on the welfare budget is the care for those unable to fully look after themselves. This is often due to advanced age, but can be due to physical or mental incapacity.

The needs of different individuals vary considerably. People who need twenty-four-hour skilled nursing care are at one end of the spectrum. This is extremely expensive to provide, and the cost can be £2,000 per patient per week. At the other end of the spectrum there are reasonably healthy individuals who may be getting on a bit. Rather than continue to have the burden of maintaining a house, perhaps long after any children have moved out, it can be attractive to move to some form of accommodation managed by others.

For the lucky ones, this can be quite grand. One use for large houses, perhaps with substantial grounds, is to subdivide them into a number of apartments. There can be shared facilities (including recreational ones), bookable rooms for guests, and staff to maintain the place. Third-agers can enjoy a splendid lifestyle in such surroundings. They can go away on holiday happy in the knowledge that their home will be secure and looked after while they are away. They will have vacated their former home, which will thereby be added to the available housing stock.

There are other forms of shared accommodation, many of them purpose built. They can provide varying forms of help, ranging from a bit of caretaking of the premises to much more, such as shopping, cleaning and mobility assistance. Those requiring more might receive various forms of help, such as dressing and meals, in their home.

Greater security, such as having someone around all the time, might require a move into a care home. There are a great many care homes, usually privately run, but often to some extent publicly funded. The sector is struggling. Partly due to modern health and safety concerns, and partly due to the reaction to some scandals relating to abuse, it is heavily regulated.

Money is tight and staffing is a problem. Some large operators of care homes have got into difficulty. The existing broad range of facilities and services will need to be expanded much further in the years ahead, to cater for an ever-increasing population of very elderly people. Here are some ideas as to how to meet the challenges.

Very careful thought needs to be given to the question of who should pay for what. There are three main categories of expenditure: medical needs, accommodation and general household expenses (such as food and clothes). A country committed to the NHS is supposed to be committed to the provision of free healthcare for all. This is not being fully delivered to those within the care system. Many of those are paying for healthcare, via their care home fees. Nursing homes have nurses, and this is part of the package.

In a hospital, everything is free, including the accommodation and the food. To that extent, those in a care home get a worse deal. If everyone, including those in care, is to be treated equally, the state, perhaps via the NHS, should pay in full for the medical component of the care regime (some money is currently claimable for this, but at a very low rate).

The full cost should be quantifiable (care homes know, roughly, what their money is being spent on). Secure in the knowledge that this money will be paid by the state, care home operators could expand with confidence. Their patients would have lower bills and therefore more people would be able to afford residential care. Very poor patients would continue to need additional funding, over and above their state pensions, in some cases.

The problem with this approach, of course, is likely to be its huge cost to the taxpayer. We need new ideas to increase the care options available, to increase revenue and to drive down costs. One way of levelling the playing field would be to charge hospital patients for their food. Perhaps this might, among other things, improve the food. However, many hospital stays are very brief. The administrative hassle of extracting money from patients at a time when they are not at their best is unlikely to be worth it.

Society is probably going to have to be pretty firm in requiring everyone, other than the very poor, to pay accommodation and living expenses costs in full. These are likely to be quite high in a nursing home, with its institution-style overheads. Might there be some alternatives?

The care infrastructure is short of rooms and carers. The country is full of rooms and potential carers. There is an enormous, largely untapped, resource. Many houses have one or more unoccupied spare rooms. Some of these could be rented out and occupied by those no longer able to live on their own, unattended.

The pressing need for carers of various kinds, currently met by large numbers of young people from Eastern Europe and other countries, could in future be dealt with in part by using UK-based grey power. Mature individuals are likely to have good empathy with the elderly. By undertaking some care work, perhaps on a part-time basis, they could do something fulfilling and supplement their incomes.

Not everyone will be prepared to assist with dressing and toilet needs, but some will. As at present, certain things can be dealt with by visiting carers. Others might confine themselves to the provision of accommodation, and perhaps food.

It may often prove to be the case that living in someone's home, probably in a semi-self-contained room with a bathroom, suits many people much more than the institutional environment of a care home. Friendships may develop between them and their hosts.

The management of the complex cocktail of needs and resources requires specialist expertise. In essence, the issues are health related. The best organisations to provide this are probably the big trusts that operate hospitals. They would expand the scope of their care to include care for the elderly.

There is no reason why they should not themselves go into the business of operating care homes. The market could do with big new providers. It may be that a well-organised hospital trust, operating as it should be in a competitive market (see below) could compete effectively with privately funded operations. Whether or not a trust chooses to go down this route, it should be given power to license and manage care provision of the kind described above. In doing so, it will have some of the solution to bed-blocking problems in its own hands.

The new, off-site care provision should be much more economical to run than the present structures, which they would complement. It would be a large, flexible resource providing homely care for those who need it and welcome income for those who choose to get involved.

It is not a radical idea, which makes it all the more surprising that it has been ignored so far. What is suggested in relation to (mainly) old people is very much in step with fostering arrangements for young people in the childcare system. The main difference is that, with the benefit of their state pension and perhaps other income, those cared for will be able to pay some, or all, of the (non-medical) cost.

Even once such new resources come on stream the system is likely to be under pressure. Personal care is very labour intensive. The upside is that it offers plenty of employment, but the downside is the cost. Technology may, at last, be poised to lend a hand. Often derided as the stuff of science fiction, and in practice the victim of a number of false dawns, robotics may at last be coming of age. Robots are routinely used in manufacturing. Disappointingly, they do not resemble the humanoid structures that we see in comics and films. Attempts to replicate human movement have shown it to be very difficult. Dealing with obstacles such as stairs is very problematic.

Meanwhile, computers are improving their capabilities at a bewildering rate. Advanced ones now routinely beat human world champions at demanding games like chess and Go. The troublesome business of achieving workable voice recognition of commands has largely been solved.

A breakthrough will come when advanced computer power is married to a robot undercarriage sufficiently capable of moving around a home. A robot carer would be available 24/7, would be effortlessly patient, never get tired and never need a holiday. It could keep itself up to date. It could report problems. In an age where driverless cars are soon expected, we may not have long to wait for the robot carers. What a game changer they are going to be!

Health

Like motherhood and apple pie, the NHS is revered by all. Only an eccentric (and almost certainly unsuccessful) politician would dare to challenge the fundamental benefits of an institution which has, since its formation in the 1940s, dedicated itself to the provision of free healthcare for all.

The NHS is a huge concern. It is one of the world's largest employers, along with the Chinese Army, Indian railways and Walmart. It has an annual budget in excess of £145 billion, representing nearly 18 per cent of total government expenditure. After welfare, it is the biggest call on the government's purse.

In recent years, the monolith has been broken up a bit, because the Scottish, Welsh and Northern Ireland health services are controlled by their own assemblies. There is now some divergence in practice between them.

Medical advances reflect the general rapid change in almost all fields of science and technology. Although the proportion of national expenditure devoted to health has consistently gone up, the demand for care, now that more and more is possible, always seems to outpace it. As a result, there are frequent references to the service being in crisis, with overworked, demoralised staff, patients waiting a long time for treatment, a shortage of the latest equipment and medications and overcrowded hospitals.

The news is not all bad. Life expectancy has gone up considerably since the service was founded. Since then, procedures now regarded as routine, such as hip replacement surgery, enable many to live much more active lives than would have been possible before.

There is probably a limitless demand for healthcare, and so some decisions about the allocation of resources are inevitable. Although this is generally recognised, there is a strong sense that this enormous institution could work much better than it does. But, how?

One of the things that all political parties have recognised since the war is the importance of the NHS and the huge benefits it brings to the whole of society. We are committed to the principle on which it was founded, which is that the best healthcare that the country can afford will be delivered free to patients. It is the task of government to make this as efficient as possible. The present system fails in this respect.

Although a great many highly skilled and dedicated people are working very hard within the NHS, they are hampered by an inflexible institutional approach, dogma and an unwillingness to accept changes to working practices. There are stark contrasts between the best-performing units and the worst. The system seems to lack effective mechanisms to alter this position.

Much of this is driven by politics. The NHS is cherished politically, partly because it is, in effect, our largest nationalised industry. Experience shows that nationalised industries very rarely work as well as private ones. The NHS also suffers from the fact that it is, largely, a monopoly.

We should fully embrace the market mechanism in healthcare. Market dynamics improve efficiency wherever they are allowed to operate, and it is perverse to exclude them from so vital a sector. The role of government is to create an environment in which the best approaches can flourish and manage it in the interests of patients. We should not be afraid of having different ways of doing things as we explore what works best. In commerce, flexible, agile markets work well and that is what we seek in the field of health.

There will still be a need for a great deal of government involvement. Since it will be paying for the services that patients use, it has enormous power to ensure that it gets what it wants. We should follow the principle that efficiency flows from things being done by the most junior person able to do them well. The same idea applies to physical resources, such as surgeries and hospitals. We certainly need highly skilled consultants and well-serviced hospital beds, but it is vital that these very expensive resources are only used when they are really needed.

The management of someone's health is a partnership between the patient and those caring for them. The first, and in many ways most important, carer of the patient is the patient. A great deal more can be done, from the education system onwards, to help people look after themselves via diet, exercise and other good practices. This is one way in which joined-up thinking comes into play. The municipal park and swimming pool are part of the healthcare system.

A comprehensive reconsideration of how patients can best be guided through a properly structured healthcare system is needed. It will always be complicated and expert help will need to be given by appropriately qualified professionals. Using a GP (i.e. a very highly trained person) as the sole gatekeeper to the healthcare system in order to do this is extravagant. Instead, they should expand their existing role as healthcare provision managers. As well as each patient having 'their doctor', advantage should be taken of the fact that nursing has become a largely graduate profession. Nurses, quite rightly, undertake very responsible tasks, often after receiving additional specialist training. Midwifery and mental healthcare are examples. Everyone should have 'their' nurse.

Fully qualified nurses should be perfectly capable of dealing with much of the routine work currently performed by (even more qualified, and much more expensive) doctors. They should be trusted to prescribe certain drugs, particularly where these are repeat prescriptions for chronic conditions. They should be trusted to know their own limitations and to refer cases, as needed, to a doctor.

The relationship between patient and medical provider can be a very personal one. The doctor's surgery is a place of refuge for people with all sorts of problems. Health may be the trigger for seeking help, but quite often what is needed, and looked for, is a sympathetic conversation, in confidence, with someone the patient can trust. Providing this well can deliver substantial health benefits. Problem sharing and reassurance can do a lot.

Hard-pressed GPs do their best, but do not have the time that is sometimes needed. What is more, although some of them may be technically very good, not all have the desirable patience and desk-side manner to perform this role. It is something that many nurses may be better at – particularly if they can allow more time for consultations. Some people find doctors rather intimidating, and this is much less the case with nurses. This is one obvious way in which the principle of having things done by the most junior person able to do it well can work.

Doctors, as happens now, should run their surgeries as businesses, often in quite large partnerships. They should be free to concentrate on the higher-level activities for which they have been trained, selecting and employing the right mix of nursing, physiotherapy and administrative staff to enable them to do so. The working day of a typical GP should become more fulfilling. These important roles will become a more attractive career option.

Having freed up time by employing suitably empowered nurses, GPs should be able to shoulder the burden of providing more treatment than at present, up to and including minor surgical procedures. This could be facilitated in larger practices by specialisation. Some of the load would be taken off hospitals as a result. GP-delivered treatments are likely to be much cheaper than the hospital versions, because of the inevitable huge overheads of hospitals.

We have already identified three steps on an escalator of patient care. The first is the patient. Guidance needs to be given, from school onwards, about healthy lifestyles. There needs to be awareness of how and where to get advice, including online, at a pharmacy (another underused source of professional guidance) and at the local surgery.

The patient's nurse should be a familiar and reassuring figure and often the person first consulted with a health problem. This is the second tier.

The third tier, all too often used as the first tier at present, will be a consultation with a surgery doctor. This may be the doctor identified by the patient's usual nurse as the one with the right specialist knowledge.

Even so, however capable and well-resourced a GP's surgery is, it will certainly not be able to deal with everything. Hospitals will very much be needed, so let's consider how they could function best.

Hospitals and specialist care

Modern medicine offers a huge range of treatments, provided by ever more specialised medical teams and backed up, in most cases, by ever more expensive equipment and facilities. Patients cannot be expected to identify how and when to call on these resources. This is a task for their doctor.

Some years ago, the concept of GPs operating as fund holders, using their budget to buy treatment in hospitals, was launched. The idea was to introduce a powerful market mechanism. Efficient hospital departments would attract more patients, less efficient ones would have to shape up, or wither.

Although this market-based approach is commonplace in other areas of life, its introduction into the NHS was highly controversial. As a result, much of its initial impact has been lost due to reversals of policy.

We need to reinvigorate the market idea. The existing, highly expensive public hospitals ought to be capable of attracting patients based on their quality of service. There are some private hospitals – let them compete. If, despite the need to keep shareholders happy, they can do a better job, what's the problem? The state will continue to supply treatment to patients free at the point of delivery, and it will be a demanding customer.

Given a chance, the market mechanism will raise standards, improve practices and lower costs. It will perform better than the current cumbersome regime of detailed targets and official inspections. These dispiriting mechanisms generate a lot of expensive paperwork and the associated frustration for little benefit. We have a chunk of old-style Eastern Europe operating in our midst.

A patient referred to a hospital is entering the 'fourth tier' of the treatment escalator. How can the hospital be made efficient?

Most modern hospitals are large. In the past there were a lot of cottage hospitals where local people received treatment, often from doctors who were also GPs. Increased specialisation and changes in approaches to treatments (whereby confinement to bed is reduced to a minimum) have led to their disappearance. There is also an idea that a big hospital can provide economies of scale. Some of the role of the old cottage hospitals has been transferred to larger, more capable GP surgeries.

As big organisations, hospitals employ many levels of staff, doing a wide range of jobs. There has been an explosion in the number of posts for, often highly paid, administrators. This is partly the product of the current system of target setting and assessment.

On the medical side there is a well-defined hierarchy of doctors. The most senior, the consultants, head up a team of junior doctors (some of whom are themselves very experienced), including those who have recently qualified and who rely on the regime to extend their training and experience. Because of these arrangements there is plenty of scope for things to be dealt with by those with the right level of expertise.

As with any complex organisation, bottlenecks can occur. Operations, for example, can require a team of different specialist doctors and nurses, plus the availability of an appropriate operating theatre and equipment. If just one of these is missing, the operation may have to be cancelled. Disruptions occur because of the need to cater for emergency admissions.

The art of running a hospital involves an ability to maximise the use of key people and resources. The very best keep major assets, such as operating theatres, working hard; the worst tend to find them empty on Friday afternoons ...

Hospitals deal with the fourth and higher tiers of the treatment escalator (highly complex procedures requiring the services of at least one top consultant). The NHS, and the country, can be proud that all of this, despite the difficulties and expense, is free for the patient.

The most prominent hospitals often teach medical students and are involved in aspects of research. As such, they are unquestionably major national assets. We need to make them work as well as possible and here there is obvious scope for improvement. They need to be kept match-fit via genuine competition with equivalent institutions. This should work well because those referring the patients (GPs) are experts. This mechanism would allow for the removal of a great deal of frustrating and expensive monitoring and control, and also encourage investment in the search for a competitive edge. Hospitals, like businesses, should be allowed to borrow what they need to invest. (However, care needs to be taken in future to avoid overly expensive PFI arrangements.)

A bed night in a hospital is an expensive asset. All forms of bed blocking need to be vigorously addressed. This can include hanging around for days waiting for the say-so of a consultant and the immense problem of geriatric bed blockers. Pressure on Accident and Emergency (A & E) units needs to be reduced. There needs to be much more interchange with community resources in order to achieve flexibility and efficiency.

A great deal of the above involves the huge subject of 'care'.

As far as A & E is concerned, recent years have seen this facility, designed for things like road accidents and heart attacks, increasingly used as a shortcut to treatment. There are many reasons for this. Difficulty in getting to see a GP is one. Risk-averse advice on telephone services intended to *reduce* pressure can be another. An increasing awareness that, if you are patient enough, someone will see you in A & E attracts business.

Improvements to the availability of advice away from hospital are part of the answer. A more ruthless weeding-out process in A & E departments, involving experienced nurses (backed up, in times of stress, by police officers), may be needed

Discharge into care

A major source of congestion in hospitals is the presence of large numbers of predominantly very elderly people who have finished their treatment but cannot be safely discharged. This happened to my mother. At an advanced age she had continued to live at home, with increasing levels of external support, until she fell and broke her hip. The Countess of Chester Hospital did a great job of arranging a hip replacement quickly. However, by the time she would normally be discharged, the staff were adamant that a decline in her mental condition made it impossible for her to return home. Urgent steps were taken to find a suitable care home for Mum. Nonetheless, for quite some time she was occupying a bed intended for surgical patients.

While in hospital, a large, expensive team of nurses, carers, caterers, cleaners and other staff are paid for by the state. The moment the patient moves to a care home, the position becomes much more problematic. For some, funding assistance is available from hard-pressed local authorities. Those patients with some assets have to pay, often subsidising the local authority funding in the process. In effect, this is a disguised form of taxation.

Hospitals could relieve pressure on themselves by setting up discharge centres, possibly well away from the hospital. People in the position of my mother, plus people who simply need extended convalescence prior to returning home, could be cared for there for strictly limited periods. This would free up very expensive hospital bed space and allow time for adjustment and assessment.

This idea is not new. In the days when confinement to bed in case of illness was much more common, there were convalescent homes which provided this sort of facility. The main difficulty about setting them up is probably money. Such facilities would sit uneasily in the space between fully state funded (hospitals) and perhaps not funded at all (care homes). This problem ought to be resolvable. They could charge those who can afford it for food and lodging. Hospital trusts could fund the medical care – after all, they will have freed up some of their bed space.

Education

The purpose of education is to equip people for life. It is especially important, and effective, early on. This has been recognised for many years and considerable resources have been poured into the system, providing a huge range of teaching for all ages, including the specialist education needed for specific jobs, such as nursing, plumbing, architecture … and teaching.

Schools

We have an entrenched educational establishment. It may be spending much of its time teaching the wrong things. Over 1.4 million mainly full-time staff are employed in the UK state school sector alone, over 500,000 of whom are teachers. As with the health service, something of this size can be slow moving and reluctant to adapt.

The requirement is to educate people so that they can happily play their part in a fast-moving world. It is questionable whether the subjects currently taught are all likely to best prepare people for society. It is not clear that the methods used are the most appropriate either.

Every pupil is different. The traditional 'talk and chalk' model, whereby in any class one teacher guided a group of often disparate students through the same curriculum at the same pace, hardly reflected that. Instead of 'one size fits all' teaching, an approach tailored to each individual is preferable. Until recently, it was difficult to achieve, but what about now?

Almost all youngsters are as familiar with and adept at using the controls of a tablet or smartphone as the previous generation was with its TV and hi-fi systems. This offers the prospect of a lot of independent working, online, with carefully structured teaching modules. Since these could be prepared centrally, as well as in-house within a school, they should be of high quality, interesting and flexible.

Some modules could require groups to work together and complete projects, perhaps after different lines of research had been followed. All of a sudden, pupils following such a regime would be behaving much like a work group in the outside world. Peer pressure to get things done, perhaps in the face of competition against other groups working on the same challenges, might stimulate laggards.

Boredom and the resultant disengagement are enemies of learning. They are less likely in a stimulating, flexible environment. Teaching could resemble the management of a workforce: inspiring, encouraging, assisting and evaluating. Insofar as this mirrors how the outside world works, so much the better.

Loosening up the approach to teaching widens the scope for using teaching assistants. Teaching is a profession and it is a demanding one, requiring considerable training. Such people need to be involved in guiding students through the education process. But, following the principle that efficiency flows from having things done by the most junior people able to do them well, there is much going on in schools that could be delegated to others.

One of the things that teaching assistants can bring to the mix is variety. They may be part-time, and have other jobs. In areas with ethnic or religious concentrations, they may be from different groups. They may be parents, or grandparents. They may be from other countries.

For older pupils, it could also be possible to occasionally involve people from outside the education system altogether. They might talk about their job, or they might help to devise, and then help teachers to evaluate, certain projects. Some of these might be real projects and not just exercises – setting up an allotment in an old people's home, perhaps.

The general idea behind much of the above is to prepare people to join the world outside by reducing the extent to which school is separate from it. This principle can be extended to what schools teach. There are some obvious must-haves, such as an ability to read and write, a grasp of at least basic arithmetic and, these days, computer skills. Once equipped with these, the world is your oyster.

The availability of online information diminishes the need for some of the things that were the bedrock of much education in the past, such as memorising lots of facts. Even rather simple calculations, involving long division and the like, might be viewed as optional when a cheap calculator can do it for you (if you happen to have allowed the battery on your phone to run down).

The emphasis needs to be on problem solving, creativity and learning how to find things out. Accepting that, where should teachers guide their pupils? Surely this should be in the direction of how the world works. Here are some suggestions:

- Basic geography, so that when the news comes in, you know what part of the world is being talked about.

- At least a basic timeline of history, but with most emphasis being on years within the living memory of parents and grandparents.

- Law, society and politics (this last subject is sensitive – issues need to be identified without taking sides).

- Business. (What is a company? How does marketing work? What, in general terms, does an accountant do? Who pays tax and when?)

- Perhaps most important of all, children need to become street aware, in relation to sex, relationships, online hazards, health, religions and philosophy.

In addition to the above, academic or practical subjects can be fed into the mix. It may be possible to cover a wide range of these for older pupils by taking full advantage of specialist online learning modules. Some subjects (certain languages, perhaps) may require schools to share a specialist teacher.

Education is so important that successive governments have wanted to exert considerable control over it. A number of methods are used, including directions as to what should be taught and supervision of examinations and systems of assessment.

Monitoring outcomes via exam performance is likely to remain important. Advancement to further education and employment opportunities are dependent on reliable measurements of achievement and capability. While accepting this, there should be scope for much greater flexibility than at present as to how pupils are guided towards the challenge of the various forms of standard test. Different schools could try very different methods. This would increase parental choice.

It would also allow something of a competitive market to develop. As with other markets, the best should thrive.

Competitor schools would seek to match their practices and performance.

It is possible to envisage much more inter-school pooling of resources than at present. As well as staff sharing and exchanges, they might choose to co-operate in the creation of learning modules. Particularly if these were geared to online use, they might be saleable – opening up new revenue streams for schools and sources of income for the teachers involved.

Improving education cannot be achieved simply by injecting money into the system. As with all calls on the public purse, it is in limited supply. Schools and other teaching institutions should be encouraged to help with their own economics by taking advantage of revenue opportunities. They occupy significant assets, in the form of premises, often with gyms, playing fields and other recreational facilities in addition to at least one big hall and lots of classrooms. Given the fairly short school day, weekends and long holidays, these are usually underused. A bit of imagination could combine the provision of useful community facilities with additional and often much-needed revenue.

A flexible regime, tailoring its services to individuals, under the professional guiding hands of teachers, and aiming to provide skills of obvious relevance to the modern world, has the potential to turn out a wonderful set of young adults.

Further education

When I went to university in the late 1960s only about 8 per cent of the population did. Students lucky enough to do so had confidence that, following graduation, managerial and professional positions would be readily available. So wonderful were we as a group that a grateful nation not only paid for our education there, we were given grants towards our living expenses. We responded by exploring the delights of Double Diamond beer, going on demonstrations and occasionally doing a bit of work.

The number of universities has greatly increased as various institutions have converted themselves into them, while older universities have exploded in size (from 4,500 to over 24,000 in the case of mine). Nearly half of all school leavers at least start a university course of some kind. Nowadays, they pay a lot for the privilege, often on a deferred basis via rather expensive loans.

Those who pay for things should be in a position to influence the providers. Students ought, therefore, to be able to insist on value for money in return for the considerable commitment that they have to make at a rather young age. It is still not clear to what extent the market mechanism is working, or working well, in the academic arena. Once committed to a particular course, it is difficult (though not impossible) to abandon it in favour of another one – perhaps somewhere else altogether.

At least universities have to compete for students, which must require careful attention to what they promise to deliver. This creates a tension between the need to secure enough students and the desire to maintain academic standards. There has been significant 'grade inflation' at all levels of the academic system and this extends to universities.

The university years provide a great deal more than academic qualifications and, in many ways, it is wonderful that many more people have the opportunity to enjoy them. However, there are concerns. While universities have boomed, other important learning channels have not. Compared to many other countries (Germany is often held up as an example) we are very bad at technical education in a whole range of fields such as construction, engineering, electronics and the like. Very often jobs are there, but suitably qualified people are not. This is part of the justification for bringing in workers from abroad.

As with other things to do with work, flexibility is part of the answer. There is a structure of qualification standards in the UK which properly recognises the importance and quality of a large number of vocational qualifications. Some are the equivalent of A levels and others go up the scale from there. It is perfectly possible to leave school at 16, work, gain vocational qualifications and use them as the pathway to university entrance. This combination of work experience and academic life should probably be more common than it is.

However, there may be an image problem. 'Going to uni' has some glamour to it, while an apprenticeship, however demanding, tends not to. Employers could do more to help, in their own self-interest. For example, those entering the new Dyson training facility may prove to be something of an elite – time will tell. This initiative may show the way forwards.

Going to university has never been the only way to get on in life. Getting stuck into a job in the real world a few years earlier than your student friends can pay off. Some of the world's most successful businessmen and women illustrate the point.

The police

Now named a 'service' rather than a 'force', the police play a crucial role in fostering the well-being of society. It is sometimes said that a country can be judged by the nature of the relationship between the police and its citizens. All oppressive societies rely heavily on the police to impose control by the state.

Britain has some claim to having invented the concept of the modern police force in the early nineteenth century, in Scotland, and then, in 1829, London. Prior to that, reliance was placed on private citizens organised, in the old days, by 'Shire Reeves' (sheriffs).

The British concept is that, although identifiable as professionals, police officers have powers derived from those available to all citizens (notably to arrest suspected offenders). It is true that, over time, the police have been given authority that has created considerable distinctions between them and the public. Nonetheless, the idea that the police are drawn from and rooted in the community at large is worth preserving.

This works well when the connections between those being policed and those doing the policing are strong. Recognising this, there are repeated calls for 'more bobbies on the beat', harking back to the days when patrols on foot were much more common, creating a visible street presence that reassured the public, deterred offenders and offered opportunities for interaction between officers local to the area and the public that they served.

Modern policing has to respond to a wide variety of challenges, leading to ever more specialisation and an emphasis on mobility and emergency response times. Individual officers are increasingly to be found cocooned in cars or sitting behind computer screens. This may be efficient in many ways but it does not foster connectivity with the public.

Policing becomes much more difficult when those being policed feel detached from the service, regarding it as hostile to their interests. Unsurprisingly, the flow of information from the public to the police, which is crucial to success, is likely to be choked off in those circumstances. Important recruitment of officers drawn from local ethnic groups also becomes difficult. The police become the resented 'them' and not the people 'looking after us'.

Current growing concerns about knife crime illustrate some of the problems and also provide clues to the right approach. The carrying of knives, and even guns, has become much more common as local gangs and groups, often connected to the drugs trade, engage in an arms race. When neighbourhood toughs resolve their differences by means of a punch-up, likely consequences are black eyes and broken noses. If knives or guns are used, likely consequences include deaths.

One effective way of reacting to this problem is to search those who appear likely to be carrying weapons and the police have powers to do this. However, the inevitable focus on particular areas or ethnic groups that this might involve supports a narrative that the police only target certain communities. Those searched are normally young, often black, men, and it is certainly true that, numerically speaking, they are 'disproportionately' subjected to such searches.

Nobody sane wants their area to be made unsafe by the routine carrying, and potential use, of weapons. The solution appears fairly obvious. The police need to engage closely with the people most threatened, notably by things like visits to schools. All levels of government should be involved. Following a programme of outreach to explain what is about to happen, there should be a national amnesty during which all forms of weapon can be handed in to police stations.

The amnesty should be followed by a 'blitz', in the form of intensive stop-and-search activity over a prescribed period – say, three months. As a result of earlier publicity, everyone would be aware of what was coming.

Not every owner of weapons will surrender them in an amnesty period. In one way, this is a good thing. It creates a self-identifying hardcore who can be targeted, convicted and taken off the streets. 'Blitz' programmes for major problems will work best if the affected public are on board. Greater connectivity between them and the police is highly desirable, so how might this be encouraged in an affordable way?

Drawing on the idea that efficiency flows when things are done by the most junior people able to do them well, it is clear that there is much scope for work to be done within the police service, but perhaps by people who are not themselves police officers. As police work has become more complex and specialist, officers are increasingly graduates, as well as being young, fit and able to cope with the sharper end of a workload that includes tackling violent offenders.

There is already a well-established body of special constables (part-time, civilian, volunteer police personnel) and, more recently, police community support officers. Cheaper to employ than fully fledged police, these important auxiliary staff should be well placed to form a bridge between the public and the perhaps rather forbidding police authorities. There is scope for recruiting people part-time and for using grey power. Community connections, including an ability to translate when needed, might be enhanced.

Nationalise the drug trade

One change in the law could dramatically reduce crime, improve public health and provide a significant boost to the national economy. It represents a form of nationalisation. The government could take over the illegal drug trade. Internationally, this rivals the oil industry and represents approximately 1 per cent of all global trade. In the UK alone, it is thought to be well in excess of £5 billion per year.

There are many products on the market, ranging from chemical concoctions not yet caught by the law, via cannabis, in many different forms, to cocaine, regarded as a 'harder' drug, and up to heroin. Each has its own supply chain and distribution network. Drugs are particularly dangerous because their manufacture and supply is dealt with by criminals: people hardly likely to be concerned about harmful impurities.

The unquestionable misery that drug use often causes has led governments all over the world to deploy enormous resources to try to combat the trade. Much effort by the police and even armed forces is involved. However, the long-running world war on drugs has failed. The industry continues to boom. We have not learnt the lesson of prohibition in the USA. Between 1920 and 1933 the sale of alcohol was illegal. The desire to drink it did not disappear and the consequence was that the enormous business associated with its sale passed into the hands of organised crime, creating wealthy gangs who prosper to this day (not least because they have moved into the drugs trade).

Alcoholic drink is, of course, legal for sale on a regulated basis in the UK. The tax on it produces in excess of £11 billion per year. Alcohol has considerable health risks. Drawing a distinction between it and at least the 'softer' drugs, such as most forms of cannabis, is not easy. Recognising this, some countries, like Canada, are freeing up their attitude to cannabis use.

Drugs can be addictive and hard drugs particularly so. The vast flow of money into the world of crime achieved by the trade destabilises society. The government could decriminalise use and take over and/or control supply. In doing so, all sorts of opportunities exist to eliminate particularly dangerous formulations and impurities. By selling harder drugs in controlled conditions, problems associated with dirty needles and the like can be minimised. Users can, at the point of sale, be presented with pathways out of addiction.

As with alcohol (which attracts a 'sin tax', like the one on tobacco), drugs could be taxed. Billions would flow into the exchequer. Some of the money could be used on drug rehabilitation programmes. In addition to the raw tax revenue, huge savings could result from the reduction in crime. The prison population is greatly increased by those in some way connected to the supply, or use, of drugs. Much robbery and theft is committed in order to fund their purchase.

There is a limit to the extent to which a government, however well meaning (or self-righteous), can prevent adults from doing things that they enjoy but may cause them harm. The failed attempts in relation to drug use have the disastrous consequence of transferring huge sums into the criminal economy. Legalisation as suggested would move the money back into mainstream society.

Infrastructure

Infrastructure provides the physical backbone and sinews needed for the country to work properly. It is expensive to build, maintain and keep up to date. Doing so is an unglamorous call on budgets, which are often public budgets. There is a temptation to cut corners and economise, partly because the consequences of doing so may be far from immediate. It can take years for a road to wear out or for a bridge to become weak.

Housing and real estate

Having somewhere to live is a basic need, and the availability of housing has a big influence on the way that society works. There is a shortage in the UK, because increases in population have not been matched by new building. Apart from the effect on individual living standards, this cramps the economy, as people find it difficult to live near their work, or to move to take up jobs elsewhere.

The growth of our cities can be traced like the rings of a tree. In the middle, everything is close together, suitable for an age when people moved on foot or, at the most, on horseback. There are high-density buildings, as found in Central London, in the walled cities of York and Chester and the Georgian gem that is Bath.

The arrival of railways and, later, motor transport, enabled huge physical expansion. In the case of our larger cities, notably London, this is out-and-out sprawl. The building boom between the wars created a fashion for semi-detached houses and the associated bourgeois front and back gardens –

symbolic moat-like surrounds to the little Englishmen's castles. Post-war development, still further away from the centre, has, for the most part, followed a similar pattern. The new town of Milton Keynes is built on a generous, garden-city scale. This gobbles up land. It also means that a journey to work, the shops or perhaps school requires a road trip. Except in the largest cities, public transport may not be up to the job, with the result that the roads get clogged with traffic.

We need a return to high-density, city centre housing. Unfortunately, post-war attempts at this have given the idea a very bad reputation. Up until the late 1970s there was a drive to replace units lost to wartime bomb damage and old housing stock considered to be slums with high-rise, usually council-owned blocks of flats. High-rise apartments are to be found all over the world and they can be perfectly satisfactory, even to the extent of being keenly sought after. Visionary designers like Le Corbusier planned wonderful cities in the sky, popularising the concept.

For high-rise accommodation to work well, the quality of the building needs to be very good and the choice of occupant needs to be right. It is not suitable for children, but young families have been routinely put in towers. Much worse, the build quality could be bad, leading to high-profile disasters like the partial collapse of the Ronan Point tower in 1968 and the even more shocking Grenfell Tower fire in 2017. It may be a long time before the public sector, at least, is trusted to build and manage residential tower blocks again.

Acceptable high-density housing suitable for all can be built, but we have forgotten how to do it. We just need to look at some of the most favoured (and expensive) housing in places like Belgravia (London) and Bath. Here we see well-proportioned, attractive buildings, containing about seven floors of apartments and penthouses, with generous-sized rooms. They are grouped round squares and crescents, which provide local communal space. Centrally located, they are within walking distance of shops, restaurants and other facilities. The same type of building (albeit a bit less posh) is to be found in Earls Court – one of the most densely populated areas in Europe.

High-density housing makes the provision of all sorts of services easier, because there is the critical mass of people available to make a success of facilities like shopping or a gym. Pressure on transport infrastructure is reduced.

Our cities need to stop getting flabby with ever-expanding waistlines and learn to live within their boundaries. There is a great deal of 'brown' land, in the form of previously built on space that has outlived its original use. Sometimes historic old structures (such as warehouses) can be attractively converted into desirable homes.

However, there will be times when, despite best efforts, it makes sense to build on farmland, even protected green belt (not all of which is actually green). Those who get permission to build on green belt land could perhaps be asked to buy and donate some green and pleasant land elsewhere to compensate.

An enormous amount of money is tied up in real estate, which includes a wide range of public and commercial properties in addition to housing. This store of value represents a major underpinning of the financial system. Property is considered to represent good security for bank loans.

A sudden slump in values can cause a financial crisis. However, although an increase in supply might moderate property prices somewhat, it is extremely unlikely that so many houses will be built that it causes any kind of slump. There are so many bottlenecks restricting new housing, from a straightforward lack of funds to a shortage of building land and limits to the capacities of our builders.

Housing now represents a major split between the generations. Older people have been able to sit back while their homes got ever more valuable, but equivalent homes for the next generation have become increasingly unaffordable. If the Bank of Mum and Dad is unable to resolve the problem, then perhaps the home of Mum and Dad can do so instead. Hence, the phenomenon of boomerang children who return to the nest after a period away finishing their education.

Any initiative designed to help young people buy a home runs the risk of simply feeding more money into the system and further inflating values, so the answer has to be to increase supply. Some argue that, at the same time, limitations on immigration could reduce demand.

Alternatively, homes do not have to be owned. There is a big rental sector, with units provided by private companies or individuals and housing associations. There are also a few part-ownership schemes. In addition, there is much scope for encouraging people to rent out unused rooms in their homes.

Transport

Britain's past record in the world of transport is second to none. After Britain built a network of canals to get goods moving, heroic railway pioneers like Brunel and the Stephensons made them obsolete. In so doing, they created a new technology that spread rapidly around the world, helping, among other things, to connect the Empire.

When India and Pakistan became independent in 1948, they shared over 65,000km of railway. New steamships, including Brunel's enormous *Great Eastern* – six times bigger than any previous ship – opened up the oceans and encouraged world trade. Britain ruled the waves and, for a time, had the world's biggest merchant fleet.

The First World War encouraged the rapid development of aircraft, the first of which had only flown in 1903. Britain remained at the forefront of aircraft manufacture for many years, building the Battle of Britain-winning Spitfires and Hurricanes, then, after the war, the world's first jet airliner and, in tandem with the French, the first and only supersonic passenger plane.

This history makes the present state of our transport infrastructure rather depressing. The roadbuilder Thomas Telford (another pioneer) would be unhappy at the state of many of our roads, which have been the victim of decline due to many years of underinvestment in maintenance. Even fairly basic transport upgrade projects, such as rail electrification or building new tramways, seem beset with delays and cost overruns. Heathrow, our main international hub airport, is bursting at the seams, but plans to address the problem are constantly deferred.

It is, admittedly, difficult and expensive to install new infrastructure in built-up areas and elsewhere in our crowded little island. In France, towns and cities have proved anxious to have stations on the nation's impressive high-speed rail network, whereas in the UK the emphasis is on opposition to almost any route suggested for the proposed (and astonishingly expensive) HS2 rail link to Birmingham (and in due course, further north). Getting permission for any kind of new road is similarly fraught.

We need to recapture some of the old Victorian get-up-and-go. British engineers and contractors can produce world-class projects and are much sought after as a result in the Middle East and elsewhere. Just before Hong Kong was handed back to China, they built a magnificent new airport there, joining up two islands in the process and equipping it with a state-of-the-art link to downtown. It would be nice to have similar successes closer to home. As it is, Terminal Five at Heathrow – built on time and to budget – seems to be the exception rather than the rule.

Faced with a need for airport capacity, what would Brunel do? We could expect something cutting edge and imaginative. How about an airport in the Thames Estuary, or Bristol Channel? Either would reduce overflights which currently plague built-up areas (and present the constant risk of an appalling disaster). A fast, ultra-modern communications link would be needed – so Brunel's your man. But who has his kind of vision these days?

Improving transport requires attention to detail as well as large, showcase projects. Housing needs to be near to where people work, in order to minimise commuting. Good internet connections provide their own form of communication, making some journeys unnecessary – welcome to the era of the online meeting.

Cycling, walking and vehicle sharing all have their place and need to be catered for. Exciting possibilities beckon as we anticipate self-driving vehicles, which could, among other things, transform the concept of the taxi.

Telecommunications

The British are avid users of the internet. They are, however, let down by the service provided, which is patchy and, for the most part, slow by the standards now achievable. Since the internet is vital to most aspects of modern life, including many forms of commerce, this really matters.

The position is worse in relation to mobile phone coverage. Anecdotal evidence suggests that war-torn Somalia offers better connectivity than is achieved in many rural areas in Britain. This is almost certainly true, because in some of these there is no signal at all (we rarely get one here in darkest north Wiltshire, 1 mile from the M4 motorway). This dismal performance is little short of scandalous. It is serious because it is an obvious drag on economic performance.

The problem is partly due to the legacy of a former monopoly. The telephone network was originally operated by the Post Office, which was state owned. It was the only provider. The telecoms operation has now passed to the privatised business Openreach, which has responsibility for maintaining and upgrading the system. It now faces competition, from Virgin Media and others, some of whom are now installing infrastructure of their own.

Connectivity and reliability are improving, but too slowly. The problems are partly technical and partly due to jockeying for position and market share between the old incumbent (Openreach) and its challengers. Getting telecommunications sorted out, and quickly, is the sort of national priority where the government should be actively involved.

Nationalisation is not an attractive answer, but stepping in and making sure that the rules of the game work well is required. There needs to be a massive programme of replacing old-fashioned copper cables with fibre optics, including into offices and homes. If need be, public money could be used, buying a stake in a core industry in the process (this would be one area where a sovereign wealth fund, and/or pension fund money, could work well in the public interest).

The cost of creating twenty-first-century broadband Britain is unlikely to exceed the proposed budget for HS2. It certainly looks like a better buy …

Energy

Energy takes different forms (including heat, light and motion). Electricity is a convenient way of transmitting it. Electrical generation is thus a matter of great importance. It, quite literally, powers most aspects of modern life. The eighth largest island in the world (Great Britain) is very fortunate in having more than its fair share of fuel that can be used to produce electricity. There are huge reserves of coal and the surrounding seabed has lots of oil and gas under it. Recently, it has become apparent that, in addition to some oil, there is a lot of gas under the land, trapped in rock. A new technique (fracking) is now being exploited in the USA, unleashing new sources of power. The USA is now in a position to be a significant exporter of gas.

Britain could, if it so chose, use its own reserves of coal, oil and gas to satisfy most, if not all, of its energy needs. It does not do so, because it is exercising huge self-restraint. The reason for the self-restraint is concern about the environmental impact of burning fossil fuels. Chemical pollution is one issue, but the big one is the modern worry about man-made global warming. Energy policy is based on the widely accepted idea that the carbon dioxide released by fossil fuels acts as a greenhouse gas, leading inexorably to a warming planet with potentially catastrophic results.

The consequences are immensely expensive (although proponents of the global warming theory argue that inaction would be even more so). Huge sums are being spent on enormous wind turbines, solar farms, experimental wave and tidal power schemes and other clean energy initiatives.

As a result of all this effort, significant technological advances are being made. It is likely that ever more efficient batteries will be able to store the intermittent power produced by things like wind turbines. Solar panels are getting much more efficient – and cheaper to produce. The UK is poised to generate electricity via a mix of methods, including renewable sources, nuclear power and some fossil fuels. Unless difficult carbon capture technologies can be developed, it is likely that our remaining coal will stay, unexploited, in the ground.

What about our gas? Opposition to any form of fossil fuel use is such that we are not building the new gas-fired power stations that could utilise this secure, native resource. Is it really an unacceptably dirty fuel? It is cleaner than coal. Gas and fracking will not trigger Armageddon.

We certainly need to find ways of producing electricity, because all sorts of supposedly 'green' equipment, such as electric cars, requires it. Like any resource, energy is something that we should use with care. The UK's demand for it could still be reduced by some fairly simple measures, such as better insulation of buildings, and there is scope for greater fuel efficiency in all forms of transport, including aircraft and ships.

Foreign relations

Few, if any, countries have had the UK's length and extent of involvement in world affairs. The British Empire was dismantled in the space of about twenty-five years after the Second World War, prior to which it had occupied nearly a quarter of the world's land surface, making it the biggest ever in the world by a huge margin. Its ghost survives in the Commonwealth. The Commonwealth comprises fifty-two countries, spread across all continents, and membership of this is entirely voluntary, although most former colonies choose to belong. There is little downside (and arguably little upside) in doing so.

Britain's dealings with other countries were by no means confined to empire building, of course. In Europe, at one time or another, significant wars have been fought against the French, Spanish, Germans and Dutch.

However, thanks to leading technological change via the Industrial Revolution in the nineteenth century, Britain has a long history of trade, divorced from either empire or war. There was, for example, major investment in Argentina, particularly involving the building of railways.

Where the British went, so did their language. English is the unchallenged international language of trade and diplomacy (having displaced French in the latter case, to the dismay of our friends across the Channel). Partly because of the language (shared with the USA, which is the country which in large measure supplanted Britain as a global power), Britain exerts influence through its culture. The impact ranges from Shakespeare to the Beatles.

We return to the UK's relationships with others at the end of this book.

Defence

NATO

As a NATO member, the UK is committed to spending 2 per cent of GDP on defence. It is one of very few members to do so. By contrast, the USA, still by far the world's pre-eminent military power, spends over 3.5 per cent.

A key principle of NATO is that an attack on one state is viewed as an attack on all. With a superheavyweight in the form of the USA onside, this assurance has allowed most, if not all, other members to have something of a free ride as far as defence is concerned. Germany spends about 1.2 per cent of GDP, Belgium and Spain less than 1 per cent and tiny Luxembourg less than 0.5 per cent. Fashionable politicians tend to decry the actions of the USA, as it does most of the heavy lifting, while sheltering under its huge umbrella.

In the decades after the war, as Europe reconstructed itself, this was tolerated and has become something of an ingrained habit. There are increasing signs that the USA is getting fed up with this. European leaders need to consider the extent to which it is safe to continue the old reliance on the USA and, if not, what to do. Given the many pressing demands on expenditure, there is reluctance to commit money to defence. Germany, the largest EU state, has particular reluctance as it seeks to continue to distance itself from its militaristic past. (Germany and Japan are the most pacifist significant powers in the world.)

In relation to defence, as in other issues, the UK is somewhat different from other European countries. Associations dating back to two world wars and sustained by other conflicts, from the Korean War in the 1950s to much more recent engagements in the Middle East, have tied the UK closely to the USA, albeit as an increasingly junior partner.

Even now, there is a can-do, gung-ho attitude within the British military – it is used to being on the winning side. British military capability can be regarded as a national asset in a worryingly dangerous world, so to what extent can, or should, it be sustained?

What is defence for?

The answer to this question is less obvious than it appears. Clearly no country wants to be attacked, but there are several ways of trying to avoid this. Protecting the country is about a great deal more than maintaining armed forces. Almost everything involving interaction with other countries has some relevance. There are also internal threats.

The better relationships are (which may be generated by a combination of commercial links, cultural, educational and sporting ties and a general intermingling of people), the less likely there is to be conflict. There is now recognition that 'soft power', which can be based on these links, is very important. Foreign broadcasts by the BBC are an example of a channel of soft power, but all manner of other things, including films and books, can be relevant. In the modern interconnected world, private individuals collectively have formidable and growing soft power. The influence of smartphone communication around the world is easy to underestimate, and interestingly, it is rather hard for governments to control. There is now a major new ingredient in the international relationship mix.

Old-fashioned conventional diplomacy has its place, at intergovernmental level. There are now several major international bodies, some of them specialising in particular things, which provide avenues for discussion, including informal ones. Away from mainstream government, there are numerous international gatherings of many kinds – the annual economic forum in Davos is one example.

Knowledge is power, and this very much applies in the field of defence and security. Britain's intelligence services may not accord with the James Bond model, but they are well thought of. The international dimension here is very important. In addition to the special relationship links between the intelligence personnel of the USA, Canada, Australia, New Zealand and the UK, there are separate and important links with many others. The importance of these has been underlined by the need to deal with terrorism.

Applying joined-up thinking, it can be said that military planning has to take its place as one component of a mix recognising all forms of soft power, diplomacy and intelligence.

There is one other component that has a special place in the UK's efforts: aid. The UN has set a target for annual expenditure on aid, but the UK is one of the few countries to honour this. This is a considerable, and often criticised, effort at a time when there is great pressure on the national budget. We spend 0.7 per cent of gross national income, which amounted to over £13 billion in 2016 – £1 billion of the total is distributed via the EU aid budget.

Before we can answer the question of what defence is for properly, we need to consider what threats it is required to deal with. For much of the post-war period, defence planning was focussed on the Cold War. There was a perceived threat that Russia and its Warsaw Pact allies might seek to add to the Soviet Union's immediate post-war gains via a military thrust westwards. NATO's response was to maintain significant forces in Western Europe, including the British Army of the Rhine, which was a heavily armed, fully professional force of over 50,000. In addition, the USA, UK and France developed nuclear weapons.

Following the collapse of the Soviet Union, all Western countries, with relief, helped themselves to a 'peace dividend', resulting in a sharp reduction in military spending. In the case of the UK, this reinforced a sharp downwards trajectory in the commitment to defence from the Second World War onwards. In 1947, defence expenditure amounted to 16 per cent of GDP. It reduced to 7 per cent or so in the 1950s, surging at the time of the Korean War in the early part of the decade and then gradually falling. It was just under 6 per cent in 1982 at the time of the Falklands War.

The Cold War ended in the early 1990s. The Warsaw Pact was formally terminated on 1 July 1991 and the Soviet Union formally dissolved on 26 December 1991. Reflecting this, defence expenditure fell to 4 per cent of GDP at about that time, and shrank to 3 per cent of GDP by 1997.

The current Russian leadership is smarting from its loss of status as one of two world superpowers. It has various problems. A populous and prosperous Europe lies to the west and a huge and expansionist China along the immense border to the east. Russia has an economy of modest size (it was about half that of the UK in 2016) and a population of 145 million (about one-tenth of China's).

History tells us that Russia is not a good country to try to push around. It is, however, in many ways weak, because of its geographical position and fairly small economy. In response, Russia has, in contrast to Western powers, been energetically modernising and using its military. There have been incursions into Georgia, the seizure of Crimea from Ukraine, substantial support for the pro-Russian eastern part of Ukraine with military means, active involvement in Syria and an increasingly assertive presence in the Middle East.

Applying pressure by military means is the old-fashioned way of doing things. It is not necessarily ineffective. If you are militarily strong, you can 'lean on' any country that you want to influence. Army exercises may be used as a form of unsettling muscle flexing and furtive activity by sympathisers may cultivate internal unrest. Computer hacking may create a measure of chaos. There is an outside chance that circumstances may develop which provide an opportunity for some form of intervention. A formal declaration of an aggressive war is unlikely these days, but border crossings by mysterious, well-equipped, quasi-military forces, operating in aid of rebels, can and do happen.

This is how the present situation in eastern Ukraine developed. Elsewhere, there are concerns that attempts may be made to replicate it in the Baltic states (Latvia, Lithuania and Estonia). Formerly part of the Soviet Union and with substantial Russian populations, they could be vulnerable. For the moment, the NATO guarantee is a source of reassurance. However, this to a large extent means the USA guarantee. How confident can we be that future US governments will commit to rushing to defend these countries – especially if the USA feels that its NATO allies are free-riding on defence?

Russian adventurism is one worry, but there are many others in the modern world. North Korea's nuclear threat is an obvious one, while China's claims to authority over huge swathes of international waters are another. Tensions between

India and Pakistan also simmer away. China's ambitions in the Indian Ocean and long-standing border disputes could pit the world's two most populous countries against each other. The Middle East is a constant mix of problems, involving Israel, Sunni–Shia differences and various terrorist groups. Africa and its restive populations create other concerns.

Britain and defence

Defence is an unpopular topic, almost an embarrassment, for many people. The unpleasant nature of any form of warfare is hugely off-putting. However, as with illness, hoping that it will not occur is not enough. It is important to be prepared and equipped to deal with it.

It is unwise to expect others to do difficult and dangerous things on your behalf. Unfortunately, this is pretty much where the Western powers, apart from the USA, currently are. Until fairly recently, the UK was in a better position than most. However, recent cutbacks have had a very weakening effect.

During the years of the Blair government, Britain's forces were frequently actively engaged. Over 40,000 service personnel were deployed in the First Gulf War, to remove the Iraqis from Kuwait. Considerable forces were deployed in the second, much more controversial, Gulf War and in Afghanistan. Content to strut the world stage as a result, what Blair and Chancellor Gordon Brown were not prepared to do was to provide the necessary funding. We are still trying to deal with the effects of the resultant overstretch.

Instead of overused, underfunded forces, it is desirable to have well-equipped ones that are sparingly used and only actually fighting in the case of real emergencies. While pointing out that Britain is nothing like the dominant world power that it once was, many argue that we now have no international defence role. Giving up our seat on the UN Security Council would thus be a relief – surely we can sit back and leave the expensive, difficult, dangerous stuff to others?

Can we? Should we? What would the world look like if Western powers took this view?

The uncomfortable truth is that there are few promising-looking countries able to step into the breach. The maintenance (some would say creation) of a well-policed international order, in which the rule of international law means something, is dependent on responsible countries shouldering the associated responsibilities. This gives us a clue as to where the UK's defence effort, and the activities associated with it, should perhaps be directed. We are particularly well qualified to step up to the plate. It is in our interests, and the world's, for us to do so.

We should continue to provide what Britain has managed for hundreds of years: flexible, international reach. Unlike other European states, we have never sought to maintain large land armies; the enormous ones created for two world wars were exceptional. We should not be in the business of having a big army capable of major land operations. Insofar as that is needed in Europe, this could be provided by the Germans, French and others.

Flexible world reach means being able to get to places. Large, numerous items and groups of personnel can be moved by sea. If speed is needed, then air capability does the job. A revived Royal Navy and a capable Royal Air Force equipped with good carrying capacity would fit the bill. Defence is expensive, and we cannot afford to try to be good at everything. However, we should be able to manage top-end, state-of-the-art capabilities in certain areas. Submarines, mine clearance (on land and at sea) and special forces come to mind. And then there is the nuclear deterrent. The idea of ever using it is awful beyond contemplation. But that is the point. At an annualised cost of about £5 billion over its life, it is a bargain buy. While we have it, no sane country can attack us. This would be a hell of a thing to throw away. Those who advocate doing so often tend to be those who would also oppose the immense additions to our defence budget that would be required to replicate that degree of security.

Defence personnel

Although smaller in numbers, British forces are of high quality, partly because they remain surprisingly busy. Our personnel are posted in a large number of countries, for a variety of reasons, including peacekeeping, training, diplomatic support, promoting the sale of export military equipment and relief efforts.

For much of the twentieth century, most families had connections with the military, due to the huge demands of world wars and other conflicts. National Service, which required all men (but not women) to serve in the forces for two years, only ended in the early 1960s. For some time thereafter, Britain's entirely professional services remained large by modern standards.

Today, the armed forces have been reduced to just under 200,000 people, of whom about 35,000 are voluntary reservists. The generations who were involved in the past are dying off. There is an increasing disconnect between the military and society at large.

This has implications for recruitment. Reliance on family traditions of involvement, while still helpful, is not enough. Service in the forces needs to be sold in the modern world, with its many rival opportunities. The challenge of attracting enough people with the right qualities is considerable. Britain's armed forces need to be seen to be doing a vital job well, to offer good terms of service and to equip their people with skills that are going to be useful in civilian life.

For the right people, danger and demands represent adventure and challenges and are not a deterrent. The range of skills required of modern forces, using increasingly high-tech equipment, is considerable. It is unlikely that we will be able to afford a situation whereby enough highly skilled individuals are permanently employed by the forces. A core of people with essential expertise needs to be in place, so that systems and planning are ready to respond when needed.

However, it is unrealistic to expect the forces to permanently employ lots of computer experts, logistics experts, medical staff, etc. As with many other areas of public expenditure, innovative thinking is needed to drive down cost. The recent, but as yet not very successful, move to bolster reserve forces is one good idea. It probably requires more work, in order to incentivise people and their employers to get involved.

The military, disaster relief and aid

Reservist service could be stimulated by developing a new corps within the army (or perhaps a tri-service version) specialising in one of the key functions of the modern military: disaster relief and aid.

When something awful happens such as a tsunami, earthquake, flood or civil war, the capabilities of the military become a vital part of the response. Able to react quickly and effectively in challenging circumstances and able to look after themselves, in every sense, they are in a position to achieve things beyond the capacity of civil authorities or charities (although it is clearly important to work well with both).

British forces have a very good record in providing this type of assistance. Britain still has a measure of global reach, and a large and creditable aid budget, but is no longer pretending to be a superpower, unlike the USA and China (and even Russia). We are, these days, a multi-ethnic, tolerant society. This should help to make us acceptable partners in many situations without triggering superpower rivalries. In the right circumstances, we should be able to relieve such pressures.

We can build on these attributes. In so doing, Britain can make a very valuable, possibly unique, contribution to how the modern world works. The new aid corps would have full-time personnel, perhaps sometimes on secondment from other branches of the services, and would also be a particularly good and attractive environment for part-time reservists. The corps would present a good way of re-expanding our military in a reasonably economical way while, in the process, attracting those with crucial skills. It will provide the world with a well-equipped and ready crisis-response resource.

A fast response can be crucial. In addition to aid situations, it can apply when stability is threatened due to terrorism or other forms of lawlessness. In a much-quoted example, prompt but limited action by the British Army snuffed out murderous banditry in Sierra Leone. Inaction elsewhere has allowed problems to expand alarmingly. The emergence of ISIS is, arguably, an extreme example of this.

One useful feature of expansion to create the aid corps would be the general increase in military capability that came with it. In the, one hopes unlikely, eventuality that large-scale forces were needed, this could be invaluable. Our history tells us that, in an emergency, civilians and reservists can perform very well in our forces. However, it should be emphasised that, however capable the aid corps might be, its deployment would require every bit as much care as any other military move. Working with the relevant civilian authorities, civil aid agencies and, if possible, other aid-providing countries would be essential.

The addition of an aid corps to the military mix should have beneficial, and justified, effects on the perception of our forces by the public and the world at large. One consequence might be that it could encourage recruitment.

The establishment of a well-equipped, highly capable aid corps would mean that Britain was providing a high-profile and very creditable world lead in the area.

This has to be worth it. We should not be trapped in an 'accountancy' view of aid and military expenditure, whereby the money spent is regarded as lost and unproductive. The value of such efforts may indeed be difficult to quantify in money terms, but it is undoubtedly there.

Equipment

One problem is that technology is having its impact, rendering expensive kit obsolete. Its replacement can be very costly. Military inflation tends to outpace other sorts.

Britain has been reluctant to drop hard-earned and often very good capabilities, with the result that a whole series of defence reviews (almost all geared to cost cutting) have led to salami slicing, whereby nothing is entirely abandoned, but things are shrunk.

Let's examine the requirements of one service where, in the past, Britain was pre-eminent. It was the Royal Navy that projected British power, almost unchallenged, for nearly 100 years after the Battle of Trafalgar in 1805. The expansion of the British Empire would not have been possible otherwise. As all naval officers will remind you, 70 per cent of the earth's surface is covered by water (the air force points out that 100 per cent is covered by air). A navy can project formidable and flexible power across most of the globe. With aircraft now on ships, this capability is further extended.

So, what has happened to our navy in the last few years?

It is often said that military planners equip their forces with the kit needed for the previous war. We were still building battleships (huge vessels with big guns) for the Second World War when what were needed were aircraft carriers. In the modern world there is computerisation, automation and miniaturisation. What have we just built? 65,000-ton aircraft carriers!

The preoccupation with big ships and the old way of doing things has left Britain with so few vessels that one of the main advantages of naval power – the ability to be in several places at once – has been severely compromised. We see the dismal effects of outdated thinking. We cannot afford sufficient numbers of the currently favoured, 7,000-ton, escort warships, costing up to £1 billion each.

Note also the cost of the new generation of fighter bombers for the Royal Air Force and Royal Navy. These are the F35s, a family of aircraft designed to fulfil a wide number of different roles. The programme for these is, as often happens with cutting-edge military projects, way over budget and very late. The current cost of each aircraft is a staggering £100 million, or thereabouts. We cannot afford many of them.

65,000-ton aircraft carriers, £1 billion escort ships and £100 million aircraft impose a huge strain on the taxpayer. They were conceived by people still thinking it sensible to have enormous, slow-moving, easy-to-track targets carrying manned aircraft. With the possible exception of the F35 programme, which involves many countries, these pieces of kit suffer the diseconomies of small scale, due to their limited production runs.

What might a proper twenty-first-century warship look like? Let's design one:

1) We need a much larger number of ships.

2) They need to be small, partly to keep costs down. I sailed the Atlantic in a 40-ton yacht which took part in a round-the-world yacht race. Later legs, without me on board, survived very extreme sea conditions. Small boats can be very seaworthy. Our new warship, although small, will be much larger than that round-the-world yacht.

3) In yachting, two- and three-hulled vessels are often used in demanding conditions. For technical reasons, they are usually fast (which is also desirable in a warship). They are more stable than single-hulled vessels (ditto). We should have a trimaran (three-hull) design.

4) Engines, and perhaps guns, can be mounted in the outer hulls. An anti-aircraft missile pod can be mounted in the bow of the middle hull. This more protected part of the ship can be used to accommodate the crew, which should be as small as possible. People are precious and expensive and increasingly replaceable by machines.

5) Across the stern, spanning all three hulls, there can be a deck from which to operate unmanned drones. Manned aircraft are likely to be increasingly obsolete.

6) Between the hulls there could be racks of tubes to launch cruise missiles and anti-submarine torpedoes. The inter-hull spaces can also be used to launch rigid inflatable boats, such as those used by marines.

7) The above approach would provide a new kind of small but multi-capable warship, able to go anywhere, including shallow waters. It would not need a huge crew. It would, relative to its size, be armed to the teeth, taking advantage of the fact that a ship is a much more capable carrier of weaponry than any aircraft, due to its much greater size.

8) Once the design is settled, vessels of this type could be produced in significant numbers, thereby driving down costs.

Nothing about our new warship is all that innovative but, due to what appears to be blinkered thinking, there is no sign of anything like this being considered for our Royal Navy. Nor have the possibilities of container ships been properly thought through. Often large and fast, they can carry pretty much whatever you want to put on them, provided that it is boxed up to fit. Why not develop pods of weapons, guidance systems, landing platforms and the like, ready to be plugged in at short notice in the case of an emergency need for a large ship? One or two such ships could, at any one time, operate on secondment to the navy, providing useful vessels and operational experience.

The revival of interest in lighter-than-air craft has promising implications for the military. Able to stay airborne for a long time, unlike helicopters, they have multiple potential applications, including anti-submarine and fishery protection patrols. They might be inflated on, launched from and recovered by the flight deck on our trimaran.

Our army still has heavily armoured tanks (which would have been great in 1945), heavy guns and armour-plated personnel carriers. These are the equivalents of suits of armour. How useful will this (very expensive) equipment be when modern conflicts may involve the sophisticated use of remotely controlled equipment, cyberattack and the like? Or they may involve a determined, but simply armed terrorist group.

We need modern, adaptable, agile equipment that we can afford. Our trimaran warship and part-time container warship could show the way. There also needs to be a huge amount of thinking and research about new technologies, including very small drones and computerisation.

Defence is supposed to provide security. It should be possible to 'bake in' useful security features. For example, the 9/11 disaster in New York could not be replicated if airliners were programmed not to respond to instructions to dive somewhere inappropriate. This might also prevent tragic incidents involving pilot suicides, such as the one which killed 160 people on a German Wings flight in 2015.

Brexit

Talk the talk

A country's approach to language reveals a lot about it. The French take their language very seriously. The Académie Française is charged with the task of protecting it. Attempts are made to enforce the use of 'proper French words' and to fend off the absorption of foreign ones, especially English expressions.

The approach of the British is very different. They have the *sangfroid*, the *savoir faire*, to borrow the *mot juste*, which can add a certain *je ne sais quoi* to what they want to say. English is a very absorbent, flexible, inventive language. We have no equivalent to the Académie Française.

The different ways of dealing with language reflect a different mindset, which also has an impact in the political arena. The British, open way of doing things contrasts with the French (and Continental European) desire for regulation. When there is no handy word to steal from elsewhere, it is a simple matter to invent one that works. The instant acceptance of the word 'Brexit' and its rapid adoption around the world is a prime example.

Openness, a willingness to borrow ideas and inventiveness are British characteristics. Brexit is a considerable challenge and for the UK to make a success of it we will need to draw on these qualities.

Brexit refers to Britain's departure from the European Union (EU). It is the most significant step taken by the UK since the Second World War and it is not surprising that it has generated strong views and much debate. So, what is Britain exiting from?

The EU

The Brussels Establishment is halfway towards the completion of a very long-standing, although rarely fully explained, project to seemingly create a country called 'Europe'. This may be an excellent idea – indeed, some Americans think that 'Yurp' already is one.

The origins of the EU go back to a time between the world wars when a few visionary thinkers tried to devise a way in which wars could be avoided in future. There were then few, if any, supranational bodies. The League of Nations, set up after the First World War, proved to be far too weak to prevent the second. There was no World Bank and no International Monetary Fund. International dealings were done on the country-to-country basis that had been used for hundreds of years.

The French diplomat Jean Monnet and others wanted to improve matters by having supranational bodies with genuine teeth, an ability to get things done and an ability to stop things being done – notably the commencement of wars. This was vital – hundreds of years of bloody conflicts had demonstrated that nation states could not be trusted to avoid them.

Working discreetly behind the scenes, he and a committed group of likeminded individuals devised a patient, step-by-step plan to drain power from nation states and thereby make wars difficult, and then impossible. The drive to 'ever-closer union' was enshrined in the Treaty of Rome in 1957.

(This has now been renamed with the catchy title 'The Treaty of the Functioning of the European Union'.) A moment's thought reveals what the end result of this must be: a country called Europe.

As a Frenchman who had been forced into exile in the Second World War, Monnet was particularly concerned to extinguish any possibility of yet another war between his country and Germany. To that end, he promoted the first part of his plan, which came to fruition in 1952 with the formation of the European Coal and Steel Community. Now widely accepted as the forerunner of the EU, this supranational body integrated control of what were then the core components of the industrial machine essential for modern war production. With control out of the hands of nation states, war became practically impossible.

The supranational approach had much, much further to run. The destination (a country called Europe) was rarely spelt out. The progressive accretion of power by Brussels, moving from the Coal and Steel Community to the Common Market and then the EU, has been a one-way street. Elected national governments have, over time, surrendered power to Brussels. There is not a single example of any significant power thus transferred being handed back.

Over time, the trappings of nationhood have been added. There is an EU flag, part of Beethoven's 9th Symphony does service as an anthem and, importantly, there is a common currency.

When I was practising as a lawyer in the City of London, I attended a lunch given by a group of European law firms. I was sitting next to two lawyers from Paris. The then Governor of the Bank of England, Eddie George, gave a speech about the soon to be introduced euro currency. He expressed strong misgivings.

He suggested that a 'one size fits all' currency would, given the divergent economies of the Continent, create difficulties. The implication was that the euro project was more about politics than it was about economics or common sense. My French friends laughed at him. After all, what did the Governor of the Bank of England know about finance and economics?

Further moves towards integration within the EU continue apace. They include increasing regulation of the fiscal arrangements (preventing governments from having a free hand in matters of tax and expenditure), some sort of army and a unified approach to foreign affairs (directed by Brussels).

Twenty-seven of the EU's member states seem broadly happy with this direction of travel. So, why did Britain, narrowly but decisively, choose to be different?

The referendum campaigns

Given the importance of the issue, the general standard of debate was lamentable. The British public was badly served by the political class and its associated media commentators. Its intelligence was regularly insulted.

Two prominent campaign messages illustrate the point. On the 'Leave' side it was asserted that EU membership costs the UK the eye-watering sum of £350 million per week. Outside the EU, Britain would be able to spend that money elsewhere, such as on the health service.

On the 'Remain' side, George Osborne, then Chancellor of the Exchequer, revealed the 'fact' that, in the event of a Leave vote, 'Every family in Britain will be worse off by £4,300 by the year 2030.' The Treasury, for which he was, of course, the responsible minister, said so.

Let's have a look at these propositions.

The sum of £350 million per week is, very roughly, Britain's theoretical bill for its share of the EU budget. This is, for historic and other reasons, rather bizarrely skewed in favour of agriculture and certainly not towards services (the area where the UK is strong). The resultant distortions led to vigorous action by Prime Minister Margaret Thatcher, which produced agreement that the UK would get a rebate from the gross figure of £350 million. Although part of the rebate was given up by Tony Blair without a proportionate quid pro quo, it still amounts to about £4 billion per annum. This money never leaves the UK.

Around £14.3 billion, having been provided by the British taxpayer, is sent off to be digested by the Brussels machine. However, some of it comes back to the UK. The EU, not the UK Government, decides what it is to be spent on. EU enthusiasts like Nick Clegg describe this as 'funding from Brussels'.

Once we have been the recipients of what has emerged from the digestive system of the Brussels machine there is a substantial shortfall – of the order of £9.6 billion (about £185 million per week). The money not spent in the UK goes elsewhere. One great EU success has been the absorption of former Eastern European countries and subsequent improvements to their infrastructure. A lot of the money goes there.

It can be seen that the £350 million figure which appeared on the side of the Leave campaign battle bus was misleading – many would say disgracefully so. One wonders why the (still substantial) figure of £185 million was not used instead.

Turning now to the Remain campaign's startlingly precise figure of £4,300 per household by 2030, it is hard to know where to begin with the list of absurdities it represents. Firstly, it is an economic projection. Forecasting financial events even twelve months ahead is notoriously difficult. (The Treasury has a very bad record in this respect.) Seeking to do so over a fourteen-year span is to attempt the impossible. Who knows what sort of world we will be living in then? A host of geopolitical developments, technological changes and possibly conflicts and natural disasters might occur. The reference to 'every household' was ludicrous, for the obvious reason that the circumstances of households vary enormously.

Why pick the year 2030? The presentation of this statement as having the authority of the Treasury, Britain's most important ministry, badly stained the reputation and integrity of an institution on which we need to rely. Big commercial decisions can be influenced by what it says.

To be fair, there were some more enlightening contributions to the debate, on both sides, from figures like former Foreign Secretary Lord Owen (Leave) and former Prime Minister John Major (Remain). For the most part, however, there was a lot of huff and puff, with large institutions predominantly in favour of remaining in the EU, and UKIP (whose golden hour this was) and a host of individuals across the political divide, pressing to leave.

The 17.4 million votes cast in favour of Brexit is the largest number of people that have ever voted for anything in the UK. So, what were the issues that they could base their decision on? There were four main ones: prevention of conflict in Europe, economics, governance and immigration.

The prevention of conflict in Europe

As we have seen, this has always been a prime driver of the European project. It is still regularly referred to by almost all Continental politicians. The fact that, since 1945, there has been no interstate conflict in Europe is considered to be one of the EU's crowning achievements. Opposition to the European unity ideal is regarded with bafflement for this reason.

This huge topic was a non-issue in the referendum campaign. The perception is that the chances of Britain being the subject of a military attack by an EU member state are zero. The effect of this was to remove from consideration what, on the Continent, is regarded as one of the EU's great selling points.

A country's history affects the way it views the world now. The British perspective is that we have peace in Europe because a very aggressive Germany was very decisively defeated in two world wars. The British participation in the process is recalled with pride and attempts by Continental figures to claim credit for a different dynamic are resented.

Economics

The EU is a large market with a high degree of integration. Even after Britain's population of 65 million leaves, it will still have about 450 million people in it.

The EU aims to operate and preserve four key 'freedoms' across its twenty-eight member states. They are the free movement of people, goods, services and investment. The implementation of these has had mixed results. Following the expansion of the EU as a result of the absorption of Poland,

Hungary, Romania and other former Eastern European states, there has been considerable internal migration. Most EU countries initially used a temporary provision to limit the influx, but the UK did not. As a result, the UK attracted large numbers from Poland, Romania and other countries. There are around 1 million Polish nationals in the UK and over 300,000 Romanians. There are currently about 3.5 million EU nationals living in the UK (including my wife).

There has been considerable progress in achieving the free movement of goods. The supply chains for big industries such as car manufacturing effortlessly cross national borders. This is unquestionably a success and almost certainly confers considerable advantages. Here, there is indeed a 'common market', with the associated efficiencies of the market dynamic.

There has been much less success in achieving a proper common market in the service sector. This covers pretty much all economic activity other than manufacturing, including banking and insurance, all professions, transport, tourism and much else. In 2013, a report published by the organisation Open Europe stated, 'The enquiry concluded that there is no single market in services in any meaningful sense of the term.'

There is also a patchy picture as far as freedom of investment is concerned. This is partly a product of the philosophical difference between the Anglo-American free-market model and the European 'Corporatist' one. It comes down to the familiar theme of control. In a free market, things are up for sale if the price is right. The iconic British chocolate manufacturer Cadburys was sold to the US company Kraft, but when attempts were made to buy a French yogurt company (Danone), they were blocked by the French Government, which viewed it as a strategic national asset. Major British utility companies are foreign owned. This is not the pattern on the Continent – governments there want more control over the levers of the economy.

The internal market of the EU is anything but an economic free-for-all. On the contrary, it is very, very tightly regulated. When deciding whether to buy something that involves an assessment of value, it is important to compare rival products. In order to do this well you need to know if they are equivalent. If not, a cheaper product may be less expensive for a reason.

The EU authorities want to guard against markets being flooded by shoddy goods. They certainly want to prevent the sale of dangerous ones. There is supposed to be a level field, with everyone playing by the same rules. This approach means that there need to be some rules and, boy-oh-boy, does the EU have them! The Brussels law-making machine churns them out in vast volumes (and at considerable expense). Woe betide the manufacturer who is not up to date with the latest regulations on tooth brushes or pillows (there are 109 provisions relating to pillows).

One (deliberate?) consequence of many years of this type of law making has been to create such a thicket of laws that any country seeking to extract itself is in great difficulty. We can call this the 'Brussels bindweed' problem. This is most certainly an issue for the UK. As part of its planning for Brexit, the UK is passing all of this stuff into UK law, so that, the day after departure from the EU, it will continue to be in force in the UK. Over 19,000 provisions (mostly many pages in length) are caught by this, such is the extent of the Brussels bindweed. The EU has permeated so many areas covered by government that without this process of adoption there would be chaos. Whole areas of activity would become semi-lawless.

It is, of course, ridiculous to pretend that all of the provisions covered are bad ones. What is more, in order to trade with any country, it is necessary to comply with its laws, including those relating to product standards. The EU is a very large market for UK goods and if we want to continue to sell them there, we will need to continue to observe those standards, just as goods sold to the USA have to meet the standards there. In the case of the EU, the UK is of course in an excellent position here – we instantly comply by reason of our former membership.

Given the very close – almost seamless – relationship between the UK and the other twenty-seven EU states, it would be perfectly possible for Brexit to have almost no impact on the trading relationships. Trade benefits both sides, and in the case of the EU, the UK is the second-largest recipient of its goods and services (just a little smaller than the USA and double the figure for China). The EU enjoys a surplus with the UK of the order of £80 billion, of which the German share is £26 billion. Those in favour of Brexit (Brexiteers – another useful new word) point this out and suggest that it would be madness for anyone to want to disrupt arrangements that are working rather well in the interests of all concerned.

Those opposed to Brexit (Remainers) say something curiously similar but draw a very different conclusion. They say that since the existing relationship is working rather well at present it is madness to do anything that threatens to change it. The economic advantages of continuing EU membership are sufficiently strong, and the risks of disruption following departure sufficiently great, that we should remain members.

The difference between Brexiteers and Remainers throws into relief an issue that is absolutely central to the EU project.

It has repeatedly been misunderstood, especially in the UK. This goes back to the early 1960s when a post-imperial Britain, concerned about its place in the world, started to seriously flirt with the idea of membership. The British public was told that we were seeking membership of the Common Market. As a trading nation with a long history of international commerce, this concept enjoyed a lot of support. It still does. If the arrangement was indeed about trade then, as Brexiteers suggest, there would be no barrier to the continuation of all existing trading relationships with the EU after Brexit. So, what on earth is the problem?

The problem is that the EU project seems never to have been just been about trade. Insofar as the public has been told otherwise, it has been misled, consciously or unconsciously. The EU project, above everything else, is about supranationalism. Everything must be subordinated to the drive to squeeze independent life out of nation states, and their elected governments. In this way, a new super state can be built. For those who care to look and think, this political dimension is there to see – hiding in plain sight, if you like. 'Ever-closer union' can only lead to this.

A country called Europe may be a very good idea. Indeed, many people think so. Achieving it is a major, long-term project. Progress towards it (and there is plenty of that going on at the moment) produces its own momentums and priorities, but Brexit dramatically cuts across these. It is absolutely not in the script. The political reaction to Brexit is the parent of concerns about the extent to which UK–EU trade can prosper after it takes place.

We will look at how this has an impact shortly, but for the moment we can note that worries about it lead most, although by no means all, commentators to conclude that, at least in the short to medium term, Brexit will have a damaging effect on the British economy. Some of the predictions are dire indeed.

Governance

Governance covers the system of government and the law-making process. The British system of government, like the common law, evolved continuously over hundreds of years, eventually producing the somewhat unsatisfactory, but nonetheless democratic arrangements we have now. Characteristics of the British Parliamentary approach are the lack of a written constitution, a link between geographical areas and those sent to Parliament to represent them, and the absence of PR.

The British system has been widely imitated, with varying degrees of success, mainly by many of the numerous countries that were at one time or another the subject of British rule. This includes the USA, of course, although the inspirational founding fathers there made their own contribution to institutional design by creating a written constitution modelled on the British practice, but arguably improving on it. This was coupled with the iconic American Declaration of Independence. Its 1,337 words (and the 4,543 words of the original constitution itself) are an exercise in brevity and clarity that represents an interesting contrast with the EU equivalents.

In the case of the EU, an attempt to create a constitution foundered when, in 2005, the voters of both France and the Netherlands rejected the idea by clear majorities (55 per cent against in France and 62 per cent in the Netherlands).

Following this outcome, the UK Prime Minister Tony Blair denied British voters the same opportunity. This setback to the unifying European project led Brussels to try again. Thirty months later, the Lisbon Treaty was introduced. It omitted the 'constitution' heading but contained similar provisions. The voters of France and the Netherlands were not consulted on it. It came into force in 2009. It runs to over 60,000 words.

The EU now has a complex structure involving, among other things, five presidents. There is a President of the European Council of Ministers, a President of the European Commission, a President of the European Parliament, a President of the European Central Bank and a President of the Eurozone group. The interrelationship between nation states, operating via their representatives on the council, the commission (consisting of appointed officials), the parliament and other bodies is complex.

A team of well-remunerated officials labours away in twenty-four different official languages and produces draft laws. These are processed by the Brussels machine and, if approved, emerge as either regulations, which apply across the EU without further ado, or directives, which also have to be made into law, but in the form of legislation by the parliaments of each member state. This is policed by the European Court of Justice (ECJ). If a country fails to properly do what it is told by a directive, it can be stamped on by the ECJ.

The system of directives disguises the extent to which new law is Brussels law. Since the UK and other parliaments enact them, the misleading impression is given that those elected bodies had a real role in the decision-making process. Parliament is being hollowed out. The procedural shell remains in place, but Parliament is just going through the motions. It is not possible to alter the principles set out in a directive. All that is left is a decision as to how to implement them in a UK context. A substantial amount of new UK law comes about as a result of regulations and directives, and the position is similar elsewhere. Most EU countries seem to be perfectly happy with this. In many cases, the EU law-making processes represent a considerable improvement on what they had in the relatively recent past. Some struggle to achieve workable government now. Belgium provides the EU with its effective capital, Brussels, but recently went without its own government for over 600 days due to parliamentary deadlock (produced via PR).

The Eastern European countries are shaking off the effects of dictatorial communism. Germany, Austria and Italy were in the clutches of fascism in the lifetimes of some still alive. Spain, Portugal and Greece endured spells of dictatorship. Even France went through a succession of unsatisfactory short-lived governments under the Fourth Republic, eventually opting for another model built around a very powerful presidential figure, initially in the person of De Gaulle.

In an echo of the age of Napoleon and, prior to that, strong kings, France has a tradition of decisive rule from the centre. This is bolstered by the attentions of an administrative elite – graduates of the École Nationale d'Administration. Most presidents, regardless of party, and a high proportion of others in powerful positions are members of this priesthood. Their involvement in running France provides an interesting parallel to the way in which EU officials work. The ethos of an administrative elite which controls things is to be found there too. Some refer to the resultant government by unelected officials, largely insulated from influence by the public, as 'managerialism' – a new political term to rank alongside socialism, capitalism, etc.

One of the EU's less attractive features is its apparent disdain for popular votes. Whenever a country votes in a way contrary to the will of Brussels, it is required to think again. Ireland, Denmark and Greece have all been subjected to this process. In all cases (so far) Brussels has got its way.

There is a European Parliament. So, does that inject the necessary element of democracy?

Let's compare the law-making process of the UK as a nation state with that of the EU. The role of democracy is to translate the will of the people into functional actions by government. Legitimate power rests with the people. However, except in very limited circumstances (a small old-style Greek city state, perhaps), they cannot in practice exercise it directly. Instead, power is delegated to others. In a democracy that is done based on a popular vote, for a limited period, after which the public has the opportunity to reconsider who should make laws.

For democracy to work well there has to be a proper demos. Those seeking election should indicate what their proposed policies are. Failure to do what is promised might result in losing power and that decision rests with a coherent electorate.

The UK is identifiable as an effective demos, but what about the EU?

The European Parliament recognises that there are damaging allegations of a democratic shortfall in the EU and is anxious to rectify this by bolstering its own powers. These have certainly increased over the years, but this parliament is light years away from replicating the processes familiar to us (that of parties campaigning for a set of policies).

This lack of a demos was starkly emphasised, particularly in the UK, in the 2014 European elections. There were six people hoping to become President of the European Parliament. There was actually an attempt at parliamentary campaigning in relation to this. Various groupings in the EU Parliament supported one or other of the six. They toured a number of countries to canvass support for their groups. They appeared together on platforms in order to debate.

None of this happened in the UK. With the exception of the Green candidate, none of the six were backed by any UK party represented in the parliament. The effect was that, for the purposes of electing that president, the UK was, to all intents and purposes, out of the loop and ignored.

Note also that voters have no say at all in the appointment of the other four presidents – this matters.

As presidents tend to do, they consider themselves to be at the top of the tree, able to pronounce upon and direct important matters and speak about them on behalf of the EU on the world stage. National leaders participate at one remove, by helping to select most of the presidents and by discussing issues in the Council of Ministers.

The EU is only halfway down the path of creating a country called Europe and so national leaders retain considerable clout. However, twenty-eight leaders do not always agree. They are busy people and only meet from time to time. Meanwhile, the five presidents, the commission and the associated officials grind away at the process of government, and so where does the real power now lie?

The waning power of prime ministers is reflected in a reducing ability to insist on things (note that these may be policies that they were elected to pursue). Following the expansion of the EU to twenty-eight members, the risk of deadlock has been met by introducing a system of majority voting. An increasing amount of law can now be brought in by this method. This means that a country can have laws imposed on it against the wishes of its elected government.

As the EU moved in a more integrationist direction in the period 2009 to 2015, this happened to the UK in respect of over 12 per cent of votes (three times more than any other member state). It is difficult to imagine the USA tolerating such a situation. Why should the UK?

The workings of the EU are rather obscure and, to be frank, often dull. The detail of much of the above probably passes most people by. But voters rarely vote with reference to details; overall impressions, even instincts, count. The British are an independent-minded lot and not all that keen on being told what to do. There is an impression that we are being told what to do by Brussels a bit too much.

The message of the referendum vote is that Britain wants to operate as a country. We can make our own laws, subject to our own courts and represent ourselves on the world stage.

Immigration

The free movement of people within the EU deprives the UK of complete control of its borders, who is allowed into the country and who has the right to live here. As a quid pro quo, UK citizens similarly have the right to live and work anywhere within the twenty-seven other EU states. These freedoms have resulted in considerable flows of people over the years. There are about 3.5 million EU nationals living in the UK and approximately 1 million UK citizens in the EU.

The populations of the UK and France are similar, but France has more than twice as much land. This is reflected in population densities and has implications for things like finding space for housing and infrastructure. It is very much easier and cheaper to build a railway line in France. If England is viewed as a country, its population density is the highest in Europe, apart from micro states. There are 407 people per square kilometre compared to the Netherlands, who are next highest, with 394, although the pressures are much less in Scotland, Wales and Northern Ireland.

There is a desire to preserve valued and often productive countryside in the UK, which is reflected in strong town and country planning laws that control development. A major downside of this is to make it harder, and more expensive, to provide housing for a growing population. In addition to housing, of course, there is a demand for schools, hospitals, shops, recreational facilities and other things.

The associated pressures are not evenly spread across the country and are rarely acute in the places where our lawmakers (and media commentators) live themselves. Demands on resources are especially high in inner cities.

These factors helped to make immigration a lead issue in the referendum campaign. At one end of the spectrum of opinion there is strong opposition to almost any immigration, often on cultural and racial grounds. Concerns about immigration levels are not confined to this group. There are worries that increasing numbers of people put too much pressure on available resources. It is argued that those coming from poorer EU countries depress earnings levels. There is a generalised worry that the government has no grip as far as these issues are concerned. There is resentment among those suffering most from the problems that they are casually branded racist by members of a liberal commentariat (who tend to live elsewhere).

While very far from perfect, race relations in the UK, notably in inner city areas, are much better than generally supposed. The last anti-immigrant riots took place in Notting Hill in 1958. Since then there has been a huge, and largely peaceful, assimilation of people from all over the world, notably in our big cities. I lived in multi-ethnic Brixton for nine years, over a period that included the 1981 riots there. They were nasty but, as with the even worse Broadwater Farm riot in North London, emphatically not anti-immigrant. They were driven by feelings among many black people that they were being badly treated, particularly by the police.

Identifying concerns about immigration as significant, prior to the referendum Prime Minister David Cameron lobbied leaders of other EU member states, seeking some form of control over flows of people from the EU. He was rebuffed, on the grounds that the four freedoms were sacrosanct. More generally, his efforts to get help from his EU colleagues in the run-up to the referendum were so unsuccessful that such trivial concessions as were made were ignored in the campaign.

The immigration issue was a core one and as far as that was concerned, anyone worried about it was motivated to vote Leave.

The political dimension to Brexit

The passage towards a more integrated Europe has been a slow one, but the direction of travel has been entirely in that direction, ever since Monnet and others had their vision of what could be achieved – until now.

It may be difficult, within the UK, to fully appreciate the degree of shock and disbelief in some quarters at the Brexit decision. Almost no one in Europe thought that it was remotely on the cards. Cameron's decision to hold the referendum was dismissed as an exercise to resolve divisions within the Conservative Party.

Continental comment on the decision is revealing. Emmanuel Macron, as incoming French President, said that Britain 'was withdrawing from the world'. Others said that we are 'anti-Europe', on the grounds that wanting to withdraw from the structures of the EU can only mean that. Brexiteers are supposed to be small-minded, anti-foreigner little Englanders, with an outdated mindset. In asides betraying a distaste for popular voting, it is said that the Brexit vote was carried by the old and ignorant, while the young or educated were universally in favour of remaining in.

The UK is the EU's second-largest member (about the same as France) and its decision to go represents a considerable tear in its fabric. There is a worry that this could get worse, in particular if other member states decide to leave. The whole institution could be torn apart if that happened. Inconveniently, the UK is one of the EU's biggest funders, paying about 13 per cent of the total budget and making a net contribution of about £10 billion.

There is bemusement at Britain not being in love with an EU 'which has brought peace to Europe'. There is a lack of appreciation that Britain always has viewed the EU as a trading environment, not a grander, unifying project. In short, Britain is viewed as having acted irrationally and, as a result, has kicked its EU partners in the teeth.

At the time of writing it is not at all clear what the relationship between the UK and the EU will be after Brexit takes effect. If the emphasis is placed on the economic interests of the countries involved, then trade and other interactions should continue much as before. However, the political dimension might well trump the economic one, just as it did when the decision to launch the euro was made.

If it does, the rupture could be very damaging, at least in the short term. Britain would thereby be punished (getting a kick in the teeth back). In order to do this, the EU would suffer in respect of its dealings with its second-biggest trading partner. It would be doing the economic equivalent of standing still and repeatedly punching itself in the face.

Brexit will clearly have some effect. EU spokesmen frequently speak of the EU as a 'club'. Even if we remain on close terms with its members and visit a lot, we will still not be members, helping to run it. To some degree, Britain's ties with the EU will loosen. The UK will have to look elsewhere to compensate. Some ideas as to the possibilities appear in the last part of this book. The actions of the remaining EU member states, before and after Brexit, will strongly influence the degree to which the UK remains in the general European orbit, as opposed to its traditional role as a world-class trading power. Optimistic Brexiteers think that the UK can achieve both.

Summary

1) Money controlled by individuals has an important and positive role in the operation of the economy. For this reason, we should tolerate the rich.

2) They could be taxed at high but not confiscatory levels (a maximum of 40 per cent, as applies to inheritance tax, is probably right).

3) Huge benefits would flow from a massive simplification of our ridiculously complicated tax system, not least because simplicity would eliminate loopholes.

4) Care for the elderly is an increasingly pressing issue requiring radical approaches. These could include something like the fostering arrangements already in place for children in care.

5) Hospital Trusts should play an important role in managing care, shoulder the cost of the medical component of it and liaise much more closely with outside agencies to reduce the divide between hospital care and other arrangements. This would, among other things, greatly ameliorate the serious problem of bed blocking.

6) GPs should play a major role in healthcare management on behalf of their patients, referring them to hospitals as necessary on the basis that the hospitals need to compete.

7) There needs to be an emphasis on high-quality city centre housing, drawing inspiration from the best practice in the past.

8) Infrastructure of many different types needs attention and expertise representing the modern equivalents of the Victorians. Publicly directed funding should be part of the mix and could involve sources such as pension funds.

9) We particularly need broadband and telephone connections fit for the twenty-first century.

10) In order to keep the lights on we need to avoid an overly zealous approach to energy generation. Our gas is a valuable asset that we can and should use.

11) Britain needs to remain an outgoing player on the world stage.

12) Defence and aid (which are, to some extent, linked) are part of the mix. The UK could use defence assets in support of a law-based world order. The UK can and should, in future, be a world-class deliverer of crisis response.

13) The Brexit vote puts Britain on course to a more independent future but an uncertain one. This is dealt with in the last section of this book.

4

THE FUTURE

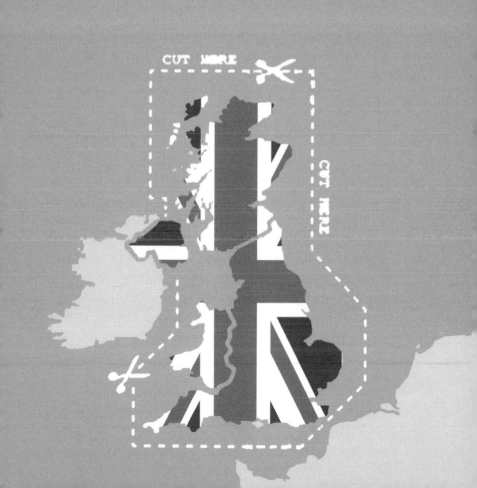

Brexit will have a considerable impact. Any consideration of what the UK might look like in the future must involve a careful look at the prospects for our European neighbours.

The conversion of the EU into a nation state is still some way off – it may never happen. Those seeking to achieve it fear that, as with cycling, a lack of progress will mean that the whole thing falls down.

However, it seems unlikely that Europe will stand still in its present form. The euro has repeatedly shown signs of being in difficulty, due to the fact that it is the currency used by sharply divergent economies. Greece and Germany are at opposite ends of the spectrum, but instability has been evident all over the place, touching Spain, Portugal, Ireland, Italy and even France. Extraordinary actions by the leader of the European Central Bank (one of the five presidents) may have done no more than defer huge problems. Greece, for example, owes debts that it will not be able to pay; much bigger Italy frets at the economic restrictions that their membership of the euro involves.

The response to difficulty in Europe is usually to call for 'more Europe'. In other words, acceleration down the path of integration. It may be that events are nearing a roadblock. Unless there is a pooling of resource (as would be normal within a country), the financial problems may be incapable of resolution. In practice, the solution (or block) is the position of Germany. Is it prepared to write off huge loans to fellow member states?

It is possible that, for the first time in the evolution of the European project, a decision will be taken to step back? This could involve a reversion to the common market concept. There might still be a closely supervised regulatory regime, possibly still involving a European Parliament in its development. But the EU would become a grouping of sovereign nation states. As such, they might co-operate externally – to collectively negotiate trade deals, for example – but would not be obliged to do so. An acid test of a reversion to sovereignty would be an ability, on the part of members, to do their own external deals if they so choose. The institutions of Brussels would shrink significantly, and the considerable powers currently vested in unelected officials such as the President of the Commission would go. All major decisions would be taken by elected governments.

If the EU converted to this model then there is little doubt that the UK would be happy to be a member, even if the Brussels bindweed was a bit constricting. However, while not impossible, this sort of retrenchment is unlikely. The slow, but relentless steamroller-like progress to ever-closer union may rumble on.

What might its final destination look like?

'Europa'

Europe is a continent. Its boundaries are a little debatable, but are normally taken to include part of Russia, the whole of Ukraine, Belarus, Georgia and certain other countries in the east, including part of Turkey. To the west, it extends to Iceland and probably Greenland, due to Greenland's continuing association with Denmark. (Greenland has become progressively less attached to Denmark and ceased to be a member of the EU in 1985.) Certain clearly European countries, such as Switzerland and Norway, are outside the EU.

On reflection, it would be inappropriate, even rude, to call the promoted entity currently called the EU 'Europe'. 'Europa' better fits the bill.

Although the EU and its predecessors have been inching towards statehood, crossing the threshold following a complete marriage of member states would still be a very dramatic development. It is likely that a period of further convergence will be required. Then there would have to be something significant enough to trigger the move to nationhood.

There are various possibilities. One or more additional countries might leave. The remaining core of enthusiast members could then decide to unite. There might be some disaster or military crisis which provides the impetus.

Don't forget Marx. The real driver of events is economics. The most probable reason to create Europa is money.

Few things have absorbed so much time, anguish and money in EU affairs as the question of keeping the euro going. A whole book can be written about the tribulations of Greece alone (and many have been). Despite all this attention, the fundamental problems have not been solved. Greece is bust. It cannot pay back what it has borrowed. This situation needs to be recognised eventually. Moreover, it is not the only eurozone member with deep structural problems in its economy.

Germany is both the problem and the solution. It is, by some margin, the biggest creditor and therefore the problem. It has Europe's biggest economy. It is a founder member of the European unifying project and a leading enthusiast for it. Nervous, for historical reasons, about fully flexing its power in the open, it prefers to work with others – all the more so because, within the EU, it can normally call the shots. The impression that it makes decisions and the French then announce them may not be fanciful.

Debt issues will come to a head sooner or later. There will either be a clear default, resulting in a damaging split threatening the whole European model, or some sort of grand bargain.

The formation of Europa

Germany enjoys huge benefits from its EU membership. If it had retained its own currency, its exchange rate would be much higher than the euro. This would be a burden for a country dependent on selling its manufactured goods. As it is, these are competitively priced, both within and outside the eurozone. Italian car manufacturers, for example, are taking on German competitors who enjoy this advantage.

The management of the eurozone, its bank and the operation of the EU generally suit Germany very nicely, but they do not equally meet the needs of other economies caught by the same rules and decisions. If managing itself, a country like Greece could allow the value of its currency to fall, pay back debt in devalued drachmas, sell its goods at attractive prices and host hordes of freely spending tourists attracted by the weak currency. These actions are blocked. Following a whole series of rescue deals, the ability of the Greek Government to decide anything at all is greatly restrained. As a result, elections in the cradle of Western democracy are rather meaningless.

As all sorts of enthusiasts for the European project point out, what is needed is a pooling of resources and debt. This is how a country works. To date, this has been strongly resisted by Germany on constitutional as well as economic grounds. These will be tough to crack. Nonetheless, given enough of a crisis, resulting in a choice between a break-up or biting the bullet and effectively writing off huge sums, Germany might well plump for the latter.

After all, it's only money. And money which, for the most part, has almost certainly been gone for a long time.

A big new treaty would be needed to set up Europa. As the paymaster effectively coming up with most of the money, Germany would be in an excellent position to design the constitution. This would build on what was there before. There is a parliament, a Council of Ministers (who are elected in their own countries), a federal-level court system and a set of countries with their own parliaments. In addition, there is a body of powerful officials.

The constitution for Europa is likely to give the impression that relatively little had changed. This would be misleading. It is inconceivable that national leaders would abandon the considerable powers that they still have with no quid pro quo.

One thing very likely to change is the European Parliament. At present, this is a haven for politicians from small countries and also-rans from big ones. Once Europa becomes a country, the big hitters will want to run its governing body. The parliament would become the fount of Europa federal law. This would, as a result, bring that more under the control of elected politicians and drain power away from officials, notably the President of the Commission.

Europa would not need the commission in its present form. The government would rely on its Council of Ministers, operating as a cabinet, and, like civil servants elsewhere, the role of officials would be to do what they are told. This would make a big change from the present position, whereby the President of the Commission (currently Mr Junker) tends to behave as the top person in Europe.

Budgetary control would be exercised from the centre and Germany would drive a hard bargain when the relevant mechanisms are put in place. Part of the point of Europa, for Germany, would be to instil appropriate financial discipline, via a strong Bundesbank-style federal authority.

The old national governments would become regional governments. The political also-rans would migrate there. They would almost certainly handle a great deal – health, education, transport, policing and much else – along the lines of the Scottish Parliament. They may retain some revenue-raising powers (which the Scottish Parliament now has). They would, however, be very constrained as to what they could do. Financial discipline within Europa would require this. More generally, the flow of regulations and directives from Brussels is unlikely to diminish.

The operation of Europa

One danger of creating a vast new country formed from many nations with different circumstances and traditions (e.g. twenty-four languages) is that government would be far removed from control by the people. No doubt there would be elections, supranational party groupings, campaigns and other features associated with the democratic process. Almost certainly, following the standard Continental practice, there would be PR.

How likely is it that Europa's democracy would work well? Coalitions would be the norm, as is already routine on the

Continent. Although these have the potential for the useful pooling of different ideas, they also have the drawbacks that we have already considered. Whatever parties offer by way of policies in an election campaign is almost certainly not going to be put into practice. Lowest common denominator government may occur.

Populations familiar with the (often complicated) political flows in their own country might find it hard to engage with the federal politics of Europa. Key ministers, handling issues like finance, foreign affairs or security might not speak in their language. Oxygen would drain from things like televised political debates. This is important – these are part of the fabric of political life.

Disengagement and apathy on the part of the electorate, stemming from a sense that there is nothing much that voters can do to influence things, would be very corrosive. A largely unaccountable political elite would then run things. This is not a desirable state of affairs. Sooner or later, there would be a reaction to it, and in the absence of effective channels to deal with the pressures, this could be explosive.

Disengagement may not occur. Voter attention might be sparked by all sorts of things. Regional tensions might arise, as politicians draw attention to differences between north and south, or east and west, or Protestant and Catholic. Whether the politics of Europa and a sufficient sense of nationhood would be up to the job of resolving these is problematic.

It is almost certain that the old national names would survive and that they would be attached to parliaments that continued to run things. They would, however, be pale shadows of their former selves, operating under federal control of budgets and the usual Brussels bindweed.

These weakened entities would be prone to disintegration. Under Europa's umbrella, breakaway movements in many European countries would gain traction. The list of candidates is long. It includes Catalonia, the Basque country, Northern Italy, Wallonia and Flanders, Bavaria and some other German Lander. This might, to some extent, be a positive development, bringing the administration of many of the functions which affect people's lives closer to the population.

Europa would be huge. Like everything else that is bulky it would have an ability to trundle on, even if run rather badly. However, the world is changing very fast. Agility and flexibility will be big advantages. How agile and flexible could the government of Europa be?

Europa could be big, but flabby. It might seek to preserve its internal organs via ever more regulation while trying to insulate itself from the athletic demands of competition in the world outside via protectionism. Such a Europa could no doubt survive and plod on, but unexcitingly.

However, the future of Europa might be very much brighter than this. The EU contains some wonderful countries, world-class businesses, first-world education and infrastructure. As Britain shows, a complex combination of cultural inputs can work well. No one thinks that the EU as it currently stands is the final version. More development is coming. Its present condition might be likened to an adolescent, suffering from immaturities and growth pains.

Having attained the equivalent of adulthood, Europa might have successfully dealt with the considerable challenge of smoothing the differences between very different national economies and cultures, in the process creating a genuine sense of cohesion and a workable demos. Such a country could be confident and outward looking and a major and valued player on the world scene. It could also be an excellent neighbour for the UK.

To get to this state, one of the things it will be essential to resolve is communication. Floundering on with twenty-four languages will perpetuate big barriers. Europa needs to look around for a useful language already widely spoken within it in the worlds of politics, education, science and the chattering classes. It would be immensely helpful if this was also the language routinely used internationally in the world of business.

Europa on the world stage

Part of the thinking behind the EU project is that, in the modern world, size is good. The USA remains the world's biggest economy (despite having a population a bit smaller than post-Brexit Europa). China, with its 1.4 billion people, comes next. India (poised to have even more people than China within a generation) is likely to gain in strength. South America and perhaps Central America may become more cohesive and represent another economic power centre.

There is no doubt that if and when the USA engages with the EU in relation to economic matters, it is taking on an entity of similar size and clout. Although it has dominant players in vital industries, like Microsoft, Facebook and Amazon, they face regulation, investigation, limitations and sometimes fines from the European authorities. In other areas, European champions challenge US dominance (as happens in the case of oil, pharmaceuticals and aircraft manufacture).

No country serious about trade would be able to ignore Europa. If trade agreements are concluded between all the super-giant players, this would cover most of the world's commerce. The EU is bad at concluding trade deals. After many years of struggle, it finally managed to do so with Canada (hardly the most problematic of counterparties), and even then, many years of tortuous negotiation nearly came to nothing due to the need to get the consent of numerous entities, including the prickly regional parliament of Wallonia. The EU has no free trade agreements at present with the USA, China or India.

Europa, as a nation state with a federal government in charge of external affairs, could be in a position to be much more decisive. That is, provided its complex internal politics, responding to disparate regional pressures, allows it.

Nation states like the USA, China and India, together with almost all others, have their own armed forces. As a country, Europa would presumably seek to do the same. Here, in contrast to its undoubted economic power, Europa's starting position would be as something of a weakling, particularly so when compared to the USA and an increasingly confident China.

Since the Second World War, Europe has enjoyed a pretty good free ride under the defence umbrella of the USA. This has been combined with disdain for and criticism of the USA in many quarters, by those uncomfortable about the use of its power. Sooner or later something will change. The creation of Europa might trigger it. Would the new country be a NATO member? If not, this would bring an end to that alliance, one effect of which would be to widen the Atlantic divide.

Even with Europa in NATO, it would be surprising if it did not come under strong pressure from the USA to step up to the plate as far as defence is concerned. This would be difficult for Europa to achieve. Germany, its dominant component, is extremely reluctant for force to be used. I was in Germany on business when the First Gulf War started to remove the invading Iraqi Army from Kuwait. The German reaction was one of horror and opposition. The contrast to the British view (which was that Kuwait needed to be liberated and that we were prepared to help) was dramatic.

Whether Europa, with its very varied traditions and historically restricted defence budgets, could ever create a military capable of facing down countries with a more robust attitude to the use of force is doubtful. Russia, in particular, is likely to test the waters. Would Europa, like North Korea, be a nuclear power? The only constituent country with this capability at the moment is France. Would all the (currently independent) countries be happy to join that club? There is strong opposition to the idea in many places.

The creation of Europa would probably impact on the United Nations. The structure of the UN Security Council has been frozen since its creation in 1945, since when the world has changed significantly. The current five permanent members are still the USA, China, France, the UK and Russia. Other countries participate for limited terms and have some voting power, but these five have the real authority – notably the power to veto actions. The emergence of Europa might be the catalyst for a shake-up. One obvious move would be for Europa to inherit France's position. Once change of this kind is in the air, others might follow. The UK has for some time adopted the position that it is time for India to join the top club – partly because of its sheer size and partly because it is something of a counterweight to China.

Particularly against the background of the UK's shrinking military capacities, its own position at the top table might come under threat. (But perhaps not – there are steps the UK could take to ensure that it makes a weighty contribution.)

More generally, a rethink of how the UN's most important body functions is well overdue. The world would be transformed for the better if the Security Council started to wield something of the immense power and influence that its members could bring to bear in support of international law and a peaceful world order. At present it is normally hamstrung due to disagreement, big power squabbling backed up by the negative threat of vetoes and a reluctance to deploy their military forces on UN missions.

Reforms could include the enlargement of the roster of permanent Security Council members. Transformation would be achieved by moving to majority voting.

The wider world

Is the world a bad news story?

We view the world partly via travel (nothing beats direct experience) but largely through the prism of news. While useful, it is important to be aware of the scope for incomplete reporting and distortions. Most deliverers of news provide their own perspective, often for political purposes.

'News' is normally something that is remarkable. The cat that did not get lost is not news. The one stuck up a tree in a town centre, rescued at inconvenience and expense by the fire brigade, is. Partly because of this emphasis on the unusual or worrying, news is predominantly bad. Modern twenty-four-hour media are able to scour the world for stand-out stories. Reports of disasters, conflicts, epidemics and murders, wherever they occur, can be beamed into our living rooms and onto our smartphones.

The process is reinforced by a plethora of interest groups and lobbyists, pressing the case for this and that, in the process predicting dire consequences if their demands are not met. In the UK, the run-up to every national budget announcement is preceded by intense activity of this kind.

There is often a good basis for the stories. It is very difficult, for example, for the NHS to meet all of the demands placed on it. It is therefore easy to find distressing cases that highlight failings – more bad news. Millions of NHS treatments each year are successful – not news.

Over time, the battering delivered by bad news, both home and abroad, can generate gloom. So, taking things in the round, should we be gloomy?

We are on a planet which will suffer conflict, disease and natural disasters. We are, however, privileged to be members of the species able to do something about these and other problems. How are we getting on? There are grounds for optimism. Whatever you think about, a case can be made for the idea that things are getting better – sometimes in fits and starts, sometimes smoothly, often unobtrusively.

Poverty, while still a huge issue, is reducing. Famines, which killed tens of millions as recently as the last century, are rare. Diseases like TB and measles are in retreat, smallpox has been defeated altogether and polio may soon be as well. The world's ability to fight a potentially devastating epidemic in challenging circumstances was put to the test in the

Ebola outbreak in 2014 – after some difficulty, it coped. Life expectancy and quality of life is improving for most people.

Education has been transformed for the better thanks to the wonderful exchange of information and ideas provided via the internet. The same mechanism should encourage an awareness of differences around the world, which, with a bit of luck, will both promote tolerance and encourage assistance of all kinds across boundaries.

In the twenty-first century, there is a growing sense of us all living in a small, connected world. In 1938, no less a figure than the British Prime Minister Neville Chamberlain dismissed a crisis in Czechoslovakia as 'a quarrel in a faraway country between people of whom we know nothing'. It would be unthinkable for any successor to say anything like that now. Whenever there is a real crisis, due to floods, earthquakes, disease or war, there is the expectation of a strong international response to help put things right. It is not always ideal or fully effective, but some form of aid is almost guaranteed (contrast this with the failure to deal with the Irish Potato Famine in the nineteenth century).

The sense of connectedness is also seen in the political arena. Leaders of the G20 countries (the ones with the largest economies) make some sort of show of trying to plan the world economy and to work together to cope with crises such as the 2008 financial crash. Since this dialogue is to their mutual benefit, it is likely that it will continue and be more effective over time.

There is talk of globalisation. It normally refers to international trading mechanisms, but it really covers everything. We are all on the same globe. Globalisation comes with the territory.

Cogs in the machine

Relations between states for trade and other things are complex. They can involve a large number of states, of varying size, doing different things. It is like a gearbox. Some cog wheels are large, others smaller, some often used, others less so, some designed to work closely together, others only occasionally engaged. Part of the challenge of international relations is the difficult one of trying to ensure that the cogs work smoothly, without an unpleasant and damaging crunching of gears. Diplomacy and other forms of contact can oil the wheels.

Major parts of the machine are easy to identify. The USA, China, India and almost certainly the EU will be pivotal to performance. There are many others in the mix.

Where might the UK fit in?

A country called the UK

The Anglosphere

What is 'the Anglosphere'?

There is no clear definition. There is certainly no political entity recognisable as such. The very idea of an 'Anglosphere' is often, partly for this reason, dismissed as a fantasy irrelevance, favoured by backwards-looking people nostalgic for elements of an empire that are now irretrievable.

Nonetheless, evidence of Anglosphere influence is all around us. English is the unchallenged language of business. The common law is the world's leading legal approach, especially for the purposes of international business and within countries which are, or pretend to be, democracies.

'Anglosphere culture', much of it, but by no means all, derived from the USA, is very pervasive, all the more so because of the online dominance of huge American firms.

A look at the map of the world can be a misleading guide to relationships. This particularly applies to the UK. We have far more in common with Australians and New Zealanders, who live on the other side of the world, than we do with the French, who are just a few miles away.

Is there any useful mileage in Anglosphere thinking, as Britain charts its future, and if so, what?

Any moves in this connection will need to be based on a hard-headed appreciation of modern realities. Those who say that yearnings for old-style empire, or even Commonwealth leadership, are misplaced anachronisms are right. But is it right to conclude that very obvious shared characteristics are therefore useless and of no importance?

Attempts to build relationships within the Anglosphere will only bear fruit via twenty-first-century thinking. Initiatives by the UK may be viewed with initial suspicion. It must be made clear that any revival of past relationships will be dealings between equals. The time has come for this. It may not have been possible in the 1960s, when the legacy of the old imperial ties was still recent and, in some cases, raw.

Another issue is that, in the 1960s, Britain made a conscious choice to sever old ties with countries like Canada, Australia and New Zealand (all of whom had loyally come to Britain's aid, a generation earlier, in a world war) and jump into bed with European countries, including Germany and Italy (who we were fighting in that war). Following on from that, the citizens of EU member states, such as Romania and Bulgaria, have free access to the UK, while those from, for example,

Australia, do not. If leaving the EU is a kick in the teeth for our European partners, remember that we did much the same to those close to us in the 1960s.

Building something concrete via the Anglosphere will only make sense, and be possible, if it is advantageous to those involved. Let's see if it might be.

If we consider which countries in the world are most like the UK, we might identify Ireland as a special case and then move much further afield. Canada, Australia and New Zealand then come to mind. One common geopolitical feature we share with these countries is the proximity of a big and potentially dominant neighbour. In the case of Canada it is the USA, for Australia and New Zealand it is China, and for us it is the EU. Each country must, in its own interests, strive for good relationships of all kinds with these influential neighbours. However, as substantial countries in their own right, none of them will want to be so absorbed by them as to lose their identity and freedom of action. (One could say that this urge for independence is part of our legacy, or at least a typical feature of Anglosphere countries.)

What other relationships might these countries have that improve their situation and mitigate against total reliance on their relationship with their neighbour?

Let's get radical. If Canada, Australia, New Zealand and the UK was a country ('New Auscanland'?) it would be the world's third-largest economy and the world's third-strongest military power. It would be the largest country in the world by area, with enormous natural resources. It would have unique territorial reach. Clearly democratic and with fully compatible legal systems and business structures, it could have considerable cohesion. Because of time zones, it would be the country which never sleeps. It would certainly be no tiddler.

'New Auscanland' is not going to happen. All of the countries concerned are happy enough in their own skin. Nonetheless, many of the benefits of such a link-up are achievable without prejudicing the clear national identities involved. They can come about via a conscious effort to co-operate across the board in trade, diplomacy, education, scientific research, defence, involvement in outer space, aid, environmental issues and much else. Following Brexit, huge possibilities open up.

The elephant in the Anglosphere room is the USA. The 'New Auscanland' countries already share highly confidential security links with this superpower. Acting in concert, rather than individually, they will be best placed to foster all sorts of other links as well. The incentive for the USA to respond constructively to them is considerable – although powerful, the USA is far from being the most loved nation around.

There is another elephant. India is on track to become the world's most populous country. Its population is already well in excess of 1 billion, although China has, so far, eclipsed it in terms of economic development. The Chinese economy is about five times the size of India's. India's relationship with China is likely to emerge as one of the big geopolitical issues of this century. China's reach is expanding very rapidly. In addition to making claims over the South China Sea, it is starting to treat the Indian Ocean as something of a 'Chinese lake'. In addition to moves in Sri Lanka, the Chinese presence is very evident in places like the Maldives.

India might feel that it is being encircled. It already has a tense relationship with Pakistan. Recently, a pro-Chinese government has come to power in the buffer state of Nepal. India itself is stirring. Held back for many years by a busy democracy devoted to outmoded socialism, overregulation and protectionism, it is now seeing the benefits of harnessing the undoubted entrepreneurial flair of its best businessmen. As a result, it is likely that India, as well as China, will be the economic success story of the twenty-first century.

In order to achieve this, India needs to migrate to a first-world way of doing things. In order to achieve that, India will need a great deal of help, if it is to close the gap with China. The 'New Auscanland' countries are excellently placed to provide this. As in the case of dealings with the USA, co-operative approaches may work better than individual efforts.

The Anglosphere is enormous. It embraces most Commonwealth countries. I was in Sri Lanka not long ago – a country with a population of over 24 million. It is growing up fast and foreign investment is flooding in. The Chinese are building a huge, obtrusive radio tower in the capital, Columbo. They are building hotels there. They are building, and taking a long lease on, a new port area. The local papers fret over the extent of all this. Travelling around, I constantly saw advertisements for 'English English' courses.

Countries like Sri Lanka are potentially fertile ground for 'New Auscanland' involvement. Are we taking advantage at present? Or of the similar opportunities emerging in Africa? Are we content to leave it all to the Chinese? If so, what are the long-term implications?

The UK and the world: business

As one of the world's largest economies (considerably bigger than Russia's, for example) the UK is a useful part of the machinery of business, but far from being a dominant one. Departure from the EU and our earlier disengagement from Commonwealth countries are bruising experiences. We cannot expect favours. We need to play to our strengths and offer mutually beneficial relationships.

Some salesmanship and confidence building will be required. This will take place against competition from others with a different world view. The French, for example, seem to think that Brexit represents an excellent opportunity for them to take over important slices of UK business, notably in financial services. Protectionist EU measures will be used to encourage this.

Critics of Brexit sometimes portray it as a withdrawal from the world ('pulling up the drawbridge', to quote Nick Clegg). This, were it to happen, would be disastrous. It would also be contrary to what Britain has been about throughout its history. Far from retreating into our shell, we need to rediscover the old merchant adventurer spirit. Part of the attraction of a trading bloc like the EU is the comfort and reassurance that an enclosed market provides. We will, to at least some extent, be stepping away from that, out into the cold.

The effect should be bracing. For the most part, our significant international trade is done by big businesses. At the time of the referendum, most of these strongly backed the Remain side. There was an element of timid clinging to nurse for fear of something worse about this.

There is a suspicion that some of our exporters have become a bit lazy and complacent. It is a bit like a football team that keeps playing in a familiar league. It may be a pretty good outfit but having to take on more exotic competition from further away can be a shock, as it is necessary to come to terms with different ways of doing things. The UK has plenty of first-class businesses who ought to be fully capable of spreading their wings internationally. The world is bristling with opportunities, including in countries finally starting to develop after a long period of struggle.

Although the UK can offer an extensive range of saleable products on world markets, this is not our principal strength. Our economy is dominated by services. Here, wherever you look, we have world-class offerings. Take your pick from banking, insurance, shipbroking, accountancy, law, management consultancy, all forms of construction and engineering, all forms of media, medicine, pharmaceuticals, almost all forms of academic research, education, almost all forms of design, outsourcing services of all kinds, IT development, intellectual property development, advertising … The UK is the world's second-largest exporter of services.

The UK and the world: international relations and security

Within the EU, the UK has its hands tied. It is not possible to conclude trade deals independently and other forms of independent action are constrained or frowned upon. Meanwhile, the EU bolsters its own representation on the world stage, behaving increasingly like a country in the process.

Liberated from these restrictions, all sort of possibilities open up. The 'Anglosphere' is worth a look. However, relations with any group, or country, do not have to have the inward-looking, restrictive character of the EU. We can seek 'as well as' links, rather than 'we'll operate solely in a huddle with you'.

This is important as new international players make their presence felt. China is impossible to ignore, but there are many others. South America (something of a no-go area for British business) requires attention. So do big countries in the Far East, like Vietnam, Indonesia and the Philippines. Opening up links will require careful, co-ordinated effort. Recent shrinkage of the UK's once impressive diplomatic service needs to be reversed and influential tools such as foreign language versions of the BBC's respected news services encouraged.

Britain has a recognisable profile, but it needs to be built on. US-funded TV series which misrepresent the doings of our royal family should not have the field to themselves. We need to behave as, and be seen as, good, reliable, helpful people to do things with.

It is here that our still excellent armed services can play a useful role. Carefully deployed, if possible with allies, they can add much-needed, first-world-standard military muscle to enforce UN resolutions. Here, there is good scope for Anglosphere co-operation, preferably involving India but not the ever-controversial USA. A reformed and reinvigorated UN Security Council could, at long last, provide effective means of enforcing international law. Failings in this respect at present militate against the whole idea of a law-based world order. A new aid corps could lead the way in showing how to deal with natural disasters.

We need the confidence to feel that the world is a better place because the UK is in it. If we get things right, others will agree.

What does the future hold?

Some say that, having cast itself adrift from the EU, Britain is destined to decline into mediocre irrelevance, outstripped by a cohesive Europe together with all manner of emerging countries and squeezed out of markets by major trading blocs who see no need for our involvement.

On this view, the country of Chaucer, Captain Cook, Shakespeare, Jane Austen, Newton, Nelson, Wellington, Darwin, the Beatles, Tim Berners Lee ... (hundreds could go on this list) has had it.

On this view, the country that has given the world a host of inventions, a large proportion of its top sports, a high proportion of its best literature and more Nobel prize winners than any country apart from the USA has had it.

On this view, the UK itself, hitherto one of the world's oldest and most successful international alliances, may disintegrate, under pressure from nationalist parties in its constituent parts, there being no reason left to stay together.

On this view, the UK, once a magnet for international talent, will see a sharp reversal, as anyone with get-up-and-go leaves for places still engaged with advances in the world, on which the UK has turned its back.

Pessimists can ignore or dismiss the fact that we are home to some of the world's oldest and best universities, or that, when we put our minds to a project (the Olympic Games, for example), we tend to do rather well (third in the medals table at the well-staged London Games and an astonishing second in Rio in 2016).

We should not be surprised that Britain is being written off. This has routinely happened for the past 1,000 years.

We have not lost our way. We have not changed our spots. We remain an outward-looking, high-performance country with further exciting chapters to add to our long, and in many respects, highly creditable history (helping to defeat tyranny in two world wars, at the forefront of the fight to abolish slavery, quickly giving independence to countries in the largest empire the world has ever seen …).

After a period of EU-induced somnolence, when at last given the chance, a majority of Britain's population opted to restore its position as a sovereign nation, able to make its own laws, subject to its own courts and representing itself on the world stage.

This was not born of hostility to any other country. On the contrary, Britain can plan to enjoy cordial and mutually beneficial relationships with almost all. It can resume its traditional role as a champion of free trade. It can participate in and encourage many other types of co-operation, breaking down barriers and increasing understanding in the process. Dealings between countries are not zero-sum games. They can, and should, be win–win.

While not, of itself, the complete world gearbox, Britain is well placed to provide a lot of important cogs in the machinery of the world.

There are certainly big challenges ahead.

We are good at those.

SOURCES AND FURTHER READING

In an effort to make this a short, readable book, footnotes and an index have been left out.

These days, online sources are impossible to ignore – Google, Bing and other search engines operate like a library; Wikipedia, among other attributes, is a wonderful source of information; every political party and any type of organisation has a website. Information sites like fullfact.org and openeurope.org.uk are also worth a look.

Useful as internet sources are, however, nothing matches the structured read provided by a book. Here are some that I found useful:

For general background as to how political life works, the three-volume diaries of former MP and minister Chris Mullin are hard to beat: *A View from the Foothills* (2009), *Decline &*

Fall: Diaries 2005–2010 (2010) and *A Walk-On Part: Diaries 1994–99* (2011).

Among the useful books offering ideas as to the future of the political left are *What's Left?* by Nick Cohen (2007), *Chavs* by Owen Jones (2016) and *Postcapitalism – a guide to our future* by Paul Mason (2015).

Those looking for background on the emergence of the British will find it in *The Tribes of Britain* by David Miles (2006).

A barnstorming, upbeat view of what we have contributed to the world is *How We Invented Freedom and Why It Matters* by Daniel Hannan (2013).

A much more critical view from the perspective of British involvement in India is Shashi Tharoor's *Inglorious Empire: what the British did to India* (2017). Following the current fashion of applying modern standards to the deeds of yesteryear, according to this, it was awful in almost every way. A counterpoint to some of the thrust of this is the 'What have the Romans done for us?' section of Monty Python's film *Life of Brian* (1979). At the very least, the effects were mixed. The British certainly fell in love with the place.

A very detailed account of the evolution of the European Union is given in *The Great Deception* by Christopher Booker and Richard North (2005). This is a book that really does get into verification via footnotes.

An astonishing account of the Royal Navy's involvement in the Second World War is Corelli Barnett's *Engage the Enemy More Closely* (1999). At one and the same time, it is a compelling narrative, an insight into the times, a view of how the military works and an impression of what can be achieved via naval power. It also shows what the Brits are like when under pressure.

It is standard practice for former prime ministers and others to write their memoirs. Often these self-justificatory tomes are of primary use to dedicated researchers and those finding it difficult to get to sleep at night. Some of the interest is in what is not said. The index to Tony Blair's *A Journey* (2010) has numerous references to his sidekick Alastair Campbell, but none to the Commonwealth. His successor, Gordon Brown, arch-devotee of expensive PFI schemes, fails to mention them.

Finally, TV, radio, broadsheet and other newspapers, and publications like the *Economist* and the rather more irreverent *Private Eye*, are fruitful sources of information and ideas.

You may also enjoy …

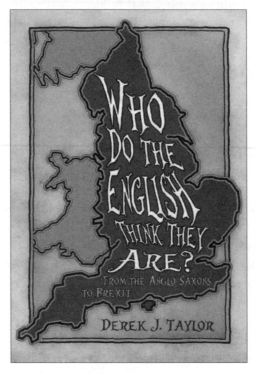

978 0 7509 8915 2

A nation's character is moulded by its history, and Derek J. Taylor is travelling the length and breadth of the country to find answers.

Now, faced with uncharted waters post-Brexit, what is it in their national character that will help guide the English people?